DATE DUE

APOKRIMATA

APOKRIMATA

DECISIONS OF SEPTIMIUS SEVERUS ON LEGAL MATTERS

TEXT, TRANSLATION, AND
HISTORICAL ANALYSIS
by WILLIAM LINN WESTERMANN

LEGAL COMMENTARY
by A. ARTHUR SCHILLER

NEW YORK, 1954

COLUMBIA UNIVERSITY PRESS

COLUMBIA BICENTENNIAL EDITIONS AND STUDIES

The Energetics of Development
BY LESTER G. BARTH AND LUCENA J. BARTH

New Letters of Berlioz, 1830–1868
TEXT WITH TRANSLATION, EDITED BY JACQUES BARZUN

On the Determination of Molecular Weights by Sedimentation and Diffusion
BY CHARLES O. BECKMANN AND OTHERS

LUIGI PIRANDELLO: *Right You Are*
TRANSLATED AND EDITED BY ERIC BENTLEY

The Sculpture of the Hellenistic Age
BY MARGARETE BIEBER

The Algebraic Theory of Spinors
BY CLAUDE C. CHEVALLEY

HENRY CARTER ADAMS: *The Relation of the State to Industrial Action*
AND *Economics and Jurisprudence*
EDITED BY JOSEPH DORFMAN

ERNST CASSIRER: *The Question of Jean-Jacques Rousseau*
TRANSLATED AND EDITED BY PETER GAY

The Language of Taxonomy
BY JOHN R. GREGG

Ancilla to Classical Reading
BY MOSES HADAS

JAMES JOYCE: *Chamber Music*
EDITED BY WILLIAM Y. TINDALL

*Apokrimata: Decisions of Septimius Severus
on Legal Matters*
EDITED BY WILLIAM L. WESTERMANN AND A. ARTHUR SCHILLER

COPYRIGHT 1954 COLUMBIA UNIVERSITY PRESS, NEW YORK
PUBLISHED IN GREAT BRITAIN, CANADA, INDIA, AND PAKISTAN
BY GEOFFREY CUMBERLEGE, OXFORD UNIVERSITY PRESS
LONDON, TORONTO, BOMBAY, AND KARACHI

MANUFACTURED IN THE UNITED STATES OF AMERICA

LIBRARY OF CONGRESS CATALOG CARD NUMBER: 2027

GENERAL EDITOR'S PREFACE

THE MODERN UNIVERSITY has become a great engine of public service. Its faculty of Science is expected to work for our health, comfort, and defense. Its faculty of Arts is supposed to delight us with plays and exhibits and to provide us with critical opinions, if not to lead in community singing. And its faculty of Political Science is called on to advise government and laity on the pressing problems of the hour. It is unquestionably right that the twentieth-century university should play this practical role.

But this conspicuous discharge of social duties has the effect of obscuring from the public—and sometimes from itself—the university's primary task, the fundamental work upon which all the other services depend. That primary task, that fundamental work, is Scholarship. In the laboratory this is called pure science; in the study and the classroom, it is research and teaching. For teaching no less than research demands original thought, and addressing students is equally a form of publication. Whatever the form or the medium, the university's power to serve the public presupposes the continuity of scholarship; and this in turn implies its encouragement. By its policy, a university may favor or hinder the birth of new truth. This is the whole meaning of the age-old struggle for academic freedom, not to mention the age-old myth of academic retreat from the noisy world.

Since these conditions of freedom constitute the main theme of Columbia University's Bicentennial celebration, and since the university has long been engaged in enterprises of public moment, it was doubly fitting that recognition be given to the activity that enlarges the world's "access to knowledge." Accordingly, the Trustees of the University and the Directors of its Press decided to signalize the 200th year of Columbia's existence by publishing some samples of current scholarship. A full representation was impossible: limitations of time and space exercised an arbitrary choice. Yet the Bicentennial Editions and Studies, of which the titles are listed on a neighboring page, disclose the variety of products that come into being on the campus of a large university within a chosen year. From papyrology to the determination of molecular weights, and from the state's industrial relations to the study of an artist's or poet's work in its progress toward perfection, scholarship exemplifies the meaning of free activity, and seeks no other justification than the value of its fruits.

Jacques Barzun

CONTENTS

LIST OF ABBREVIATIONS

Aegyptus = *Aegyptus. Rivista italiana di Egittologia e di Papirologia.* Milan, since 1920.

AHDO/RIDA = *Archives d'histoire du droit oriental / Revue internationale des droits de l'antiquité.* Brussels, since 1952.

AP = *Archiv für Papyrusforschung und verwandte Gebiete.* Leipzig and Berlin, since 1901.

Athenaeum = *Athenaeum. Studi periodici di lettere e storia dell'antichità.* Pavia, since 1913.

Bas. = *Basilicorum libri LX*, ed. Gustavus Ernestus Heimbach et Carolus Guilelmus Ernestus Heimbach. 6 vols., Leipzig, 1833–1870; 2 supp. vols., Leipzig, 1846, 1897.

Berger, *ED* = Adolf Berger, *Encyclopedic Dictionary of Roman Law* [Transactions of the American Philosophical Society, n.s. 43, part 2, pp. 331 ff.]. Philadelphia, 1953.

BIDR = *Bullettino dell'Istituto di Diritto Romano.* Rome and Milan, since 1889.

Bruns, *Fontes* = Carl Georg Bruns, *Fontes iuris Romani antiqui, I: Leges et negotia.* 7th ed. by Otto Gradenwitz, Tübingen, 1909. Cited by number.

CGL = *Corpus glossariorum Latinorum*, ed. G. Goetz. 7 vols. Leipzig, 1888–1923.

CIL = *Corpus inscriptionum Latinarum consilio academiae litterarum Borussicae editum.* 16 vols. Berlin, since 1863.

Cod. = *Corpus iuris civilis.* Editio stereotypa, Vol. II: *Codex Iustinianus*, recog. et retract. Paulus Krueger. 10th ed. Berlin, 1929.

Cod. Theod. = *Theodosiani libri XVI, cum constitutionibus Sirmondianis et leges novellae ad Theodosianum pertinentes*, ed. Th. Mommsen et Paulus M. Meyer. 2 vols. Berlin, 1905.

Demosthenes, *Or.* = Demosthenes, *Private Orations*, text and translation by A. T. Murray [Loeb Library edition]. 4 vols. London and New York, 1936–1946.

Dig. = *Corpus iuris civilis.* Editio stereotypa, Vol. I: . . . *Digesta*, recog. Theodorus Mommsen retract. Paulus Krueger. 15th ed. Berlin, 1928.

Gaius = *Gai Institutionum commentarii quattuor*, ed. E. Seckel et B. Kuebler; 8th ed. cur. B. Kuebler. Leipzig, 1939.

Hermes = *Hermes. Zeitschrift für klassische Philologie.* Berlin, since 1866.

Inst. Iust. = *Corpus iuris civilis.* Editio stereotypa, Vol. I: *Institutiones*, recog. Paulus Krueger, 15th ed. Berlin, 1928.

Isocrates, *Or.* = Isocrates, *Orations*, text and translation by George Norlin and La Rue Van Hook [Loeb Library edition]. 3 vols. London and New York, 1928–45.

JEA = *Journal of Egyptian Archaeology.* London, since 1914.

JJP = *The Journal of Juristic Papyrology.* New York and Warsaw, since 1946.

Leges = *Leges*, ed. Salvator Riccobono [*Fontes iuris Romani antejustiniani, pars prima*]. 2nd ed. Florence, 1941. Cited by number.

Meyer, *Jur. Pap.* = Paul M. Meyer, *Juristische Papyri: Erklärung von Urkunden zur Einführung in die juristische Papyruskunde.* Berlin, 1920. Cited by number.

Mitteis, *Chrest.* = Ludwig Mitteis and Ulrich Wilcken, *Grundzüge und Chrestomathie der Papyruskunde*, II Band: *Juristischer Teil*, II Hälfte: *Chrestomathie.* Leipzig and Berlin, 1912. Cited by number.

Mitteis, *Grdz.* = Ludwig Mitteis and Ulrich Wilcken, *Grundzüge und Chrestomathie der Papyruskunde*, II Band: *Juristischer Teil*, I Hälfte: *Grundzüge.* Leipzig and Berlin, 1912.

Mnemosyne = *Mnemosyne. Bibliotheca philologica Batava.* Leyden and Leipzig, since 1852.

Musée Belge = *Musée Belge. Revue de philologie classique.* Louvain, since 1897.

Negotia = *Negotia*, ed. Vicentius Arangio-Ruiz [*Fontes iuris Romani antejustiniani, pars tertia*]. 2nd ed. Florence, 1943. Cited by number.

OGI = *Orientis graeci inscriptiones selectae*, ed. Wilhelm Dittenberger. 2 vols. Leipzig, 1903, 1905.

Preisigke, *Fachwörter* = Friedrich Preisigke, *Fachwörter des öffentlichen Verwaltungsdienstes Aegyptens in den griechischen Papyrusurkunden der ptolemäisch-römischen Zeit.* Göttingen, 1915.

Preisigke, *WB* = Friedrich Preisigke, *Wörterbuch der griechischen Papyrusurkunden,* ed. E. Kiessling. 3 vols. and Vol. IV, part 1. Berlin, since 1925.

RE = *Realenzyklopädie der klassischen Altertumswissenschaft,* ed. Pauly, Wissowa, Kroll, Mittelhaus, and Ziegler. First series, 22 vols.; second series (A), 7 vols.; supplement, 7 vols. Stuttgart, since 1894.

Script. Hist. Aug. = *Scriptores Historiae Augustae,* text and translation by David Magie [Loeb Library edition]. 3 vols. London and New York, 1921–32.

Select Papyri = A. S. Hunt and C. C. Edgar, *Select Papyri,* Vol. II [Loeb Library edition]. London and New York, 1936. Cited by number.

SZ = *Zeitschrift der Savigny-Stiftung für Rechtsgeschichte, Romanistische Abteilung.* Weimar, since 1880.

Taubenschlag, *Law* = Rafael Taubenschlag, *The Law of Greco-Roman Egypt in the Light of the Papyri, 332 B.C.—640 A.D.* Vol. I. New York, 1944.

Taubenschlag, "Rezeption" = Rafael Taubenschlag, "Geschichte der Rezeption des römischen Privatrechts in Aegypten," *Studi in onore di Pietro Bonfante nel XL anno d'insegnamento.* Vol. I. Milan, 1930; pp. 367 ff.

Vat. Frag. = *Iurisprudentiae anteiustinianae reliquias* . . . Compositas a Ph. Eduardo Huschke, 6th ed. E. Seckel et B. Kuebler, Vol. II.2, ed. Bernardus Kuebler. Leipzig, 1927; pp. 191 ff.

Wenger, *Quellen* = Leopold Wenger, *Die Quellen des römischen Rechts* [Österreichische Akademie der Wissenschaften, Denkschriften der Gesamtakademie, 2]. Vienna, 1953.

Wilcken, *Chrest.* = Ludwig Mitteis and Ulrich Wilcken, *Grundzüge und Chrestomathie der Papyruskunde,* I Band: *Historischer Teil,* II Hälfte: *Chrestomathie.* Leipzig and Berlin, 1912. Cited by number.

Wilcken, *Grdz.* = Ludwig Mitteis and Ulrich Wilcken, *Grundzüge und Chrestomathie der Papyruskunde,* I Band: *Historischer Teil,* I Hälfte: *Grundzüge.* Leipzig and Berlin, 1912.

APOKRIMATA

TEXT, TRANSLATION
AND HISTORICAL ANALYSIS

by William Linn Westermann

RESPONSES TO INQUIRIES
PRESENTED TO SEPTIMIUS SEVERUS
AND PUBLISHED IN ALEXANDRIA

A.D. 199-200

THIS SINGLE SHEET of papyrus came to the collection of the Nicholas Murray Butler Library of Columbia University in the summer of 1930 by way of a purchase and distribution made by Sir Harold I. Bell, then of the British Museum. The remainder of the group of Greek papyri purchased in that year which came to the United States was added to the important collection of the University of Michigan.

The presentation of the text and its translation, its analysis, and the historical and juridical commentary upon it, have been the combined work of William Linn Westermann, Professor Emeritus in the Faculty of Political Science, and Professor A. Arthur Schiller, of the Faculty of the Columbia University School of Law. Mr. Westermann has assumed the responsibility for the reading of the text, its translation, the commentary upon it, and the brief sketch of its historical importance. Professor Schiller has undertaken the more exacting problem of the juridical interpretation of the decisions ascribed to the emperor Septimius Severus and his young son, Caracalla, and of placing them in the setting of the legal development of the Empire in that period.

There is no indication in the purchase report of the place in which the Columbia document was found. We have given it the publication number P. Columbia 123, in sequence after the last number, 122, in P. Col. iv (Zenon Papyri II). Nor has any possibility presented itself of identifying or placing any of the petitioners whose names appear or addresses in the replies of the emperor Severus which would give a clue to the town or city for which the Columbia copy was intended. The assumption that this copy probably came from the Fayum, possibly from ancient Tebtunis, rests upon the report made by Sir Harold Bell. According to Bell's rapid reading of the fifty-seven complete and fragmented pieces contained in the purchase and distribution of that year (1930), eleven mention the town in which the specific transaction occurred. Of these eleven, eight pieces have to do with activities in towns of the Fayum; and of these eight, the town in which that particular activity took place, in seven cases, was Tebtunis.

Caracalla's name appears with that of Severus in the heading of the Columbia *apokrimata*, with the title *Sebastos (Augustus)*. Since we know that he was only thirteen years old in A.D. 198 when that title was bestowed upon him,[1] we have constantly referred to these *responsa* as emanating from Severus alone, understanding, of course, in connection with each answer, the assistance and advice of his judicial staff, including the praetorian prefect, C. Fulvius Plautianus, which accompanied him and helped, anonymously, in formulating his decisions.

A number of examples of decisions rendered in A.D. 199–200 by Septimius Severus, in the name of himself and Caracalla as *Augusti*, have long been known from the Greek papyri.[2] P. Columbia 123 is the only one of the number now extant, however, which gives so definitely the place of publication of these imperial decisions as the Stoa of the Alexandrian Gymnasium.[3] Our document also clearly identifies itself as a series of transcripts (*antigrapha*).

In the case of P. Columbia 123 the copying was done by a practiced professional scribe. The papyrus sheet which he used seems to have had original imperfections on its surface in some places, possibly holes in other places. This is suggested by the broken spacing of the verb φρ ο ντισουσιν in line 31 and of αλ λοις in line 42, which falls almost directly below the break in *phrontisousin* above. Again, the space which separates πει θ[ο]υ in two parts, line 56, is in the same position as measured from the right edge of the sheet as that in line 31.

The copyist failed to take down the names and titles of the two *Augusti*, Septimius Severus and Caracalla. They certainly appeared upon the original list posted in the Stoa of the Gymnasium, since they were copied off on the transcript of two *responsa* of the same emperors which was published as P. Amherst 63. One of the two answers preserved in P. Amherst 63, that

[1] *Script. Hist. Aug.*, Severus, 16, 3; Paul von Rohden in *RE*, 2, 2441.

[2] All of those available at the time his book appeared were used by Johannes Hasebroek, *Untersuchungen zur Geschichte des Kaisers Septimius Severus* (Heidelberg, 1921). For those published since then, with an admirable understanding of their usefulness and the method of their use, consult E. P. Wegener's articles, "The βουλή and the Nomination to the ἀρχαί, in *Mnemosyne*, 4th Series, 1 (1948), 15–42, 115–132, and 297–325, using the references in the notes.

[3] In the broken line 4 of P. Flor. III 382, it is possible that the publication in the Stoa of the Gymnasium was included.

in lines 5–6, corresponds exactly with P. Col. 123, lines 8–10. It is clear that any copy which was taken off for citation purposes or for other use by advocates or administrative officials in the metropolis or the towns of the nomes must have the name of the emperor or that of the prefect who issued the answers concerned. The omission of the customary names and titles in P. Columbia 123 is a strange one if we envisage the copyist, as I think we must, as a professional writer of Alexandria, accustomed to hire out his services for this purpose. That he was a professional is suggested by the clarity of the writing, despite its lack of any pretense of elegance.

In the Columbia copy the names and titles of the two *Augusti* were crowded in later between the heading and the first decision taken off. The writing of this second scribe is blunt and the lettering small because the space available for the long list of the titles was otherwise inadequate for the purpose. The result is legible enough.

The copyist of the heading of the document and the imperial decisions displays a marked liking for ligatures, as in *tethenton*, line 1; in the name *Artemidoro*, line 11, *pithes thai*, line 12; *hyper allon*, line 19; *pros tous*, in line 59; and elsewhere. He omits all *iota* adscripts and shows a marked preference for *iota* alone instead of *ei* in writing the present infinitive, as in *ektinin* in line 20. Hasty transcribing is shown in his failure to estimate beforehand the length of the line, sometimes causing him to insert a syllable above the line at its end as in *keleusi* in line 17. Or he crowds the letters together as at the end of line 57. Examples of haste or carelessness are indicated by corrections upon original mistakes as shown in the change of σου to σε in line 15 and in κωλυονται in line 20. In line 26 he dropped out a syllable in *dia[ka]tochēn*.

P. COLUMBIA 123

(Inventory No. 516)

13.9 x 5.6 inches

*Posted in Alexandria
March 14, A.D. 200.*

*The copy probably came from the Fayum,
possibly from Tebtunis.*

ΕΝ ΑΛΕΞΑΝΔΡΕΙΑ

(1st hand) αντιγραφα αποκριματων τεθεντων εν τη στοα
του γυμνασιου. η (ετους) Φαμενωθ ιη. (2nd hand) Αυτοκρατωρ Καισαρ Λουκιος
Σεπ]τιμιος Σηουηρος Ευσεβης Περτιναξ Αραβικος Αδιαβηνικος Παρθικος Μεγιστος
Σεβαστος και Αυτοκρατωρ Καισαρ Μαρκος Αυρηλιος Αντωνεινος Σεβαστος.

5 (1st hand) Ουλπιω Ηρακλανω τω και Καλλινεικω.
     τας επιβληθεισας Αλεξανδρευσι η Αιγυπτιοις ζημι-
     ας δηλωθεν (τα) χρονον προσαγα[γο]ντες ανηκαμεν.
     Αρτεμιδωρ[ω] τω και Αχιλλι.
     τοις εγνωσμενοις συνκαταθεμενος βραδεως

10   μεμφη τα δοξαντα.
     Αυρηλιοις Αρτεμιδωρω και Ανουβιωνι και αλλοις.
     τοις εγνωσμενοις πιθεσθαι.
     Κιλ.[..]δις τω και Μιδα δια Φιλοκρατους υιου.
     ωσπερ ανατραπηναι την πρασιν των υποθη-

15   κων ου δικαιως αξιοις ουτως απολαβειν σε [[σου]]
     την νομην των χωρις συνβασεως κατεχομενων
                         σι.
     προς βιαν χωριων ο ηγουμενος του εθνους κελευ
    ...θαλγη Αμβρηλου δια Αβδομανχου υιου.
     αργυριον γυναικες δανιζεσθαι και υπερ αλλων

20   εκτινιν ου κωλυονται.
  [αι] ομοιως προετεθη εν τη αυτη στοα.
  Α]πολλωνι Αρνεκτωτου και αλλ[ο]ις.
     αι περι των επισκεψεων. κρισις κοινη παρεσχεν

προνοιαν Αιγυπτιοις.

25   Αυρηλιω Σαρ[α]πιωνι.
       τας γενο[μ]ενας εκ μητρωου γενους εις δια<κα>τοχην
       κατερχεσ[θ]αι πρωην εκωλυσαμεν.
       Π[ρ]οκλω Απολλ[ω]νιου.
       τους γεγρ[α]μμενους κληρονομους (και αι διαθηκαι
30   τειλασθαι λεγωνται) της ν[ο]μης ουκ εστιν
       δικα[ι]ον εκβληθηναι. φρ ο ντ[ι]σουσιν δε οι
       τα[ς] δικας επιγεγραμμενοι καλεσαι τους
       ευ[θ]υνομενους ει γε το πραγμα εστιν εν τη
       ταξει των διαγνωσεων.
35   Κρονιω Ηρακλειδου.
       αι προσκαιροι νοσοι των πολιτικων ουκ απαλλασου-
       σιν λιτουργιων και οι ασθενεις δε τω σωματι λιτουργ-
       ουσιν εαν τη φροντιδι των οικιων πραγματων
       εξαρκιν δυνωνται.
40   Κ(αι) ομοιως.
       Διοσκ[[ο]]ωρω Ηφαιστιωνος και Πιεσηϊ Οσιριος
       και αλλοις.
       αργυριον αντι πυρου καταβαλλιν υμας εκω-
       λυσαμεν.
45   Ισιδωρω Δειου.
       τα μεν απο Κομωνος τετολμημενα
       Φλουειος Πλαυδιανος ο κρατιστος επαρχος
       των στρατοπεδων και οικειος ημων
       εξετασι. προς δε Απιωνα τον τελωνην ει μη
50   κοινωνι των ενκλημ[α]των Κομωνι, τον
       ηγουμενον του [ε]θνους ε[ξ]εις δικα[σ]την.
       Ισ]ιδωρω τω και Ηρακλ[ειδ]ει [δια Α]πολλωνιου.
       της πατρωας κληρονομιας αποστας και
       την εκ της ηλικιας ου[κ] εχων βοηθειαν τω
55   νομω των πρασεων επι την ουσιαν δε-
       δημευσθαι φης. πειθ[ο]υ.
       .[.]ελαθηω Καιρενου.
       εαν τοις ορφανοις επιτροπους λ[α]βης
       εξωθεν ταξεως υπερ των χωριων προς τους
60   νεμομενους δικαστης δοθησεται.

NOTES UPON THE TEXT

1–4.   P. Amh. 63 cites the same answer to Artemidorus, alias Achilles, which appears in lines 8-10.   In P. Amh. 63 there are two minor differences in the imperial titles from the reading in P. Col. 123.   The title *Sebastos* (*Augustus*) among the titles of Severus appears after *Pertinax*.   In P. Col. 123 at the end of the lines honoring him *Eusebes* (*Pius*), which appears in P. Amh. 63 among the titles of Caracalla, is omitted in the Columbia copy. This is probably due to lack of space for it in the cramped insertion of the imperial heading.   The Amherst copy of the heading is, of course, to be considered as closer to the original than the Columbia one since it was, in the Columbia copy, a later insertion.

7.   There is space, certainly, for one letter at the end of *delothen*( ), before *chronon*; but only the slightest trace of ink, if any, is to be seen.

10.   Certainty for the reading μεμφη is derived from P. Amh. 63.   Change to μεμφει as suggested correctly by Ludwig Mitteis, *Chrest.* No. 376, l. 5.

13.   The letter *mu* may possibly be read in place of the letter dotted as doubtful after *lambda* in the broken name Cil-dis.

14.   For ως as causal, compare P. Amh. 68, l. 4.

15.   An original genitive, *sou*, has been corrected to *se* by writing an *epsilon* over the *omicron* of *sou* and carrying the bar of the *epsilon* across the *upsilon* of *sou*.

18.   There are a number of Greek names of women which begin with the adjective *Agath-*.   The temptation to insert it here, reading Agathalge, has been avoided.   The combination would mean "good misery."   Professor Adolph Grohmann of the University of Cairo has written me that the name ending in -alge may well be Semitic.

26.   The omitted noun which goes with τας γενομενας is κληρονομιας.

37.   At the end of the line the *rho* of *leitourgousin* is crowded in above the alignment.

40.   I have here expanded the large K to K(αι) as in K[αι] ομοιως in line 21.

41.   In the name Διοσκωρω the first *omega* has been written over an original *omicron*.

47.   Read Φουλοeverος Πλαυτιανος.

52.   The space is correct for the restoration [δια Α]πολλωνιου.   For the avoidance of elision, see δια Αβδομανχου in line 18.

TRANSLATION
IN ALEXANDRIA

1–4 Copies of *responsa* posted in the Stoa of the Gymnasium.

Year 8, Phamenoth 18. Imperator Caesar Lucius Septimius Severus Pius Pertinax Arabicus Adiabenicus Parthicus Maximus Augustus and Imperator Caesar Marcus Aurelius Antoninus Augustus.

5–7 To Ulpius Heraclanus, also called Callinicus.

We revoked penalties imposed upon Alexandrians or Egyptians when we assigned a definite time (of remission).

8–10 To Artemidorus, also called Achilles.

Having placed yourself in agreement with the decisions (rendered), too late you take umbrage at the judgments (given).

11–12 To the Aurelii Artemidorus and Anoubion and others.

Comply with the opinions rendered.

13–17 To Cil-dis, also called Midas, through Philocrates, his son.

Since you feel decisively that the instrument of sale of the mortgages was unjustly voided, the prefect of the province will issue the order that you regain possession of the plots seized by force without an agreement.

18–20 To -thalge, daughter of Ambrelus, through her son, Abdomanchus.

Women are not forbidden to obligate themselves for loans or to exact payment in behalf of others.

21–24 Likewise published in the same Stoa.

To Apollo, son of Harnektotes, and others.

The (edicts) regarding investigations. A general edict has given consideration to Egyptians.

25–27 To Aurelius Sarapion.

Some time ago we forbade that inheritances from the mother's side come down in succession.

28–34 To Proclus, son of Apollonius.

It is not just that the heirs written in wills—the wills may even be said to have given rise (to them as heirs)—have been ejected from their right of possession. Those who have introduced the cases will take care to summon those who are being charged if, indeed, the affair is of the type of case requiring jurisdiction of a special judge.

35–39 To Cronius, son of Heraclides.

Transient sicknesses do not afford relief from municipal liturgies.

Those who are physically sick are subject to liturgical services if they are mentally capable of conducting their household affairs.

40–44   Likewise (i.e., also posted in the Stoa).

To Dioscorus, son of Hephaestion, and to Pieseis, son of Osiris, and others.

We have forbidden that you pay money in place of grain.

45–51   To Isidorus, son of Dius.

His Excellency, Fulvius Plautianus, prefect of the camps and our household companion, will conduct the investigation of the audacious actions (emanating) from Comon.   In respect to Apion, the tax collector, if he is not involved with Comon in the charges (against him, Comon) you will have the prefect of the province as your judge.

52–56   To Isidorus, also called Heraclides, through Apollonius.

Although you gave a deed of cession in the matter of your paternal inheritance and you do not have the assistance (arising) from minority status, you assert that, under the law of sales, confiscation has been applied against your estate.   Comply.

57–60   To -elatheus, son of Caerenus.

If you take guardians for orphans outside of the (regular) order, in respect to their properties a judge of special delegation will be given against those assigned (i.e., against the guardians).

THE QUESTION OF GREEK AND
LATIN TERMINOLOGY

THE LINGUISTIC PROBLEM of P. Columbia 123 can best be approached by posing two questions. Were the advisory and judicial responses, here copied from the draft posted in the Stoa of the Gymnasium at Alexandria, originally written in Latin? Or, were they inquiries which dealt with local Egyptian situations and enchoric law? In the latter case they would obviously not be subject to direct transferences of Latin legal terms into the Greek phraseology which we have in the Columbia copy.

Certainly in the case of one answer to a request for information (lines 22–24) the original document, the over-all, or general, edict which covered the matter was written in Latin. The reference to it is, however, so general that no trace of the original Latin appears in the brief reference to it. In most of the cases the private law out of which the problem arose or the public law upon which an administrative question was based was that of the local Greco-Roman practice.

There is no support for the idea of direct translation from Latin, or for the necessity of it, to be gained from a consideration of the linguistic attainments of the emperor Severus or those of his "household companion," Gaius Fulvius Plautianus, the praetorian prefect. With both of them the Punic of Leptis Magna, the North African city of their birth, was the native tongue. Dio Cassius and Aelius Spartianus tell us that Severus was thoroughly conversant with the Greek and Latin languages.[4] His trilingual ability must have been a necessary part of his Roman military and administrative career, and it was undoubtedly refined, both in Latin and in Greek, by his periods of study at Rome and Athens.[5] A similar assumption of linguistic familiarity must be made for most of the entourage of the emperor. This decision is particularly applicable in the case of Fulvius Plautianus,[6] who had risen in the imperial *cursus honorum* to the high position of prefect of the praetorian

---

[4] Dio Cassius, LXXVI (or LXXVII). 17. 2; Aelius Spartianus, *Script. Hist. Aug.* Severus, 1, 4.

[5] M. Fluss, "Severus (13)," *RE*, 2A, 2000–2001. Hasebroek, *Untersuchungen zur Geschichte des Kaisers Septimius*, p. 191, includes in his early *cursus honorum*, in addition to his career in Rome, services in Sardinia, Africa, Spain, Syria, Gaul, Sicily and Upper Pannonia. He also made nonofficial visits to Athens in A.D. 181 and 186.

[6] P. Col. 123, 45–49.

guard. In the duties of that office knowledge of Latin would be indispensable. His command of Greek should be thoroughly attested by his designation by Severus to serve as judge in the case against an Egyptian official named Comon (lines 46–49). A similar assumption of linguistic familiarity, certainly covering both Greek and Latin, is to be made for the entire official entourages of the emperor during his activity in Egypt.

The conclusion must be that our list of imperial replies to the problems presented to the emperor Severus in Egypt offers no additions to the direct transfers, in the field of official terminology, from the Latin into the Greek which were particularly conspicuous in the second century. This decision is, for me, supported by the nature of those responses which seem to be based upon general imperial pronouncements as contrasted with the judicial decisions which would find their justification solely in the Greco-Roman law of Egypt. In my judgment the replies of P. Columbia 123, contained in lines 5–7, 11–12, 18–20, 22–24, 26–27, 35–39 and 41–44, fall in the group of general imperial edicts.

Certainty for this is found in the brief answer regarding the taking of evidence (lines 22–24). It is to the effect that "a general edict (*krisis*) has given consideration to the Egyptians."[7] A clear case of this use of *krisis* as edict of the ruling emperor appears in one of the anti-Christian certifications of the time of the Decian persecution where the meaning of "the divine edict"[8] is unmistakable as an imperial decision covering the entire Empire. In conformity with its pagan, anti-Christian character, demanding denial of Christian association or belief, the imperial order is called a "divine edict" (*theia krisis*). *Krisis* is also used in Egyptian papyri of the second and third centuries in the meaning of "the judgment," or "decision," of the Egyptian prefect. Its use in P. Columbia 123, line 23, as edict of the emperor is therefore the first example of its kind so far as known to me. The Greek *krisis koine* (general edict) of our rescript group serves as the Greek equivalent of the Latin *edictum commune*, as the adjective *commune* appears in the phrase *commune jus gentium*.

[7] In Friedrich Preisigke's *Wörterbuch* (Heidelberg, 1924–1944), s.v. κρίσις, examples are to be found of its use as "imperial edict."

[8] P. Oxy. XII 1464, 6; John R. Knipfing, "The Libelli of the Decian Persecution," *Harvard Theological Review*, 16, No. 38 (1923), 383. The *kriseis* of P. Oxy. VIII 1102, 14, of the second century and of P. Lond. Inv. 2565, 58 and 99–100, A.D. 254, published by T. C. Skeat and E. P. Wegener in *JEA*, 21 (1935), 231–232, are judgments rendered by the Egyptian prefects. In P. Oxy. VIII 1119, 18, also of A.D. 254, a clear distinction is drawn between "the divine laws" of the emperors and the judgments of the Egyptian prefects (the *theai nomothesiai* and the *kriseis tōn hegemonōn*).

In P. Columbia 123, line 7, there is another example of an equivalent phrase in the two languages, in *delothen[ta] chronon = tempus certum* of the Latin.[9] Another equivalent, rather than a borrowing, is the customary *proetethe*, line 21, which reproduces the Latin *propositum est*.

For the use of *ethnos* in line 51 with the meaning of the Latin *provincia*, see P. Fay. 20, 10–11: "in all of the cities throughout Italy and those in the other provinces (*ethnesin*)." [10] *Antigrapha apokrimaton* in the heading of the Columbia document is nothing more than the equivalent of the Latin *exemplaria responsorum*.

Kratistos egregius in P. Columbia 123, lines 47–48, as the honorary designation of the praetorian prefect is a regular usage in the imperial chancery at Rome.[11] In the official documents originating in Egypt both *kratistos* and *lamprotatos* are used in the titulary of the prefect of Egypt, with a marked preference for *lamprotatos* in reference to him from the time of the prefecture of Flavius Crispus, A.D. 180 or 181.[12]

There is a noteworthy difference in the Columbia *apokrimata*, lines 45–51, in the method of reference to the two prefects, the praetorian and the prefect of Egypt. The high position of Gaius Fulvius Plautianus is made conspicuous by his designation by name, by title of rank, by position, and by special emphasis upon his close relation to the emperor: "His Excellency Fulvius Plautianus, prefect of the camps and our household companion." In marked contrast to this the name of the current prefect of Egypt, Q. Maecius Laetus, is not given, and there is no title of rank. Only the position is mentioned "the prefect of the province." It is the praetorian prefect, also, who received the more important part of the investigation, as court of special designation in the separation of the case by the emperor in his answer to the petitioner, Isidorus, son of Dius. It is the examination of the offending higher official, Comon, which is assigned to Fulvius Plautianus. In marked contrast stands the delegation to the Egyptian prefect of the less important case against an ordinary tax gatherer. The omission of the name of the prefect of Egypt may, however, be due merely to a change in the

[9] Cod. Theod., 4.14.1, title: Actions shall be completed within a definite period of time (*tempore certo actiones finiendae*. Cf. Dig. 1.20.2; 27.1.3.

[10] Wilhelm Schubart, *Archiv für Papyrusforschung*, 14 (1941), 58; Knud Hannestad, "Septimius Severus in Egypt," *Classica et Mediaevalia*, 6 (1944), 217.

[11] David Magie, *De Romanorum Juris Publici Vocabulis* (Leipzig, 1905), p. 105; and Otto Hornickel, *Ehren und Rangprädikate in den Papyrusurkunden* (Giessen, 1930), p. 20.

[12] This preference is clearly marked in the list compiled by Arthur Stein, *Präfekten von Ägypten in römischen Kaiserzeit* (Bern, 1950), pp. 110–111.

occupancy of that office. For in year eight of Severus there were two prefects of certain record, Aelius Saturninus and Quintus Maecius Laetus, with
the strong possibility of a third between them, one Alfenus Apollinaris.[13]
Q. Maecius Laetus was certainly holding this Egyptian prefecture upon
May 23 of A.D. 200,[14] and the assignment of the case of the official, Comon,
and the tax collector, Apion, was published on April 13 of that year. The
reason for the emphasis upon the difference in rank between the two prefects
is, of course, conjectural; but the fact is there.

[13] *Ibid.*, pp. 107–111.
[14] *Studi di filologia classica*, 12 (1935), 106, line 17 (Friedrich Preisigke, *Sammelbuch* 7817).

THE SEPARATE CONSTITUTIONS[15]
OF SEVERUS

Lines 5–7

"To Ulpius Heraclanus, also called Callinicus.

"We revoked penalties imposed upon Alexandrians or Egyptians when we announced a definite time (of remission)."

A letter of February 5, 1953, from Professor Rafael Taubenschlag has been of great assistance in reaching the understanding of this rescript which we here present.

The inquiry was clearly administrative, dealing with penalties, presumably meaning monetary fines (*zemias*), imposed for reasons unexplained. The question asked by the official, Ulpius Heraclanus, had to do with fines which affected Alexandrians or Egyptians in his area of competence. The distinction to be made between administrative *responsa* and those of a judicial kind is well established.[16] Reading *delothen[ta] chronon prosagagontes*, the imperial response was based, as I see it, upon a previous general amnesty which Severus here declared applicable in the case either of the class of Alexandrians or that of the Egyptians.

There is a possibility that the penalties imposed upon the Alexandrians and Egyptians arose out of their advocacy of the imperial claims of Pescennius Niger and their support of his cause in Palestine.[17] The revoking of the punishments inflicted upon the Palestinians had occurred within the year before Severus's entry into Egypt and the issuing of this decision. The idea has here been rejected because the imperial remission applied by the emperor Severus was a general amnesty and apparently referred to long-standing monetary penalties.

[15] The general term "constitutions" is here used to cover all the imperial replies, as they are defined by Gaius 1. 5; "A *constitutio* of the Princeps is what the emperor has determined by a decree, by an edict or by letter." Cf. Ulpian in Dig. I.4.1.1: *haec sunt quae vulgo constitutiones appellamur*; Rafael Taubenschlag, "The Imperial Constitutions in the Papyri," *JJP*, 6 (1952), 121.

[16] Ulrich Wilcken, *Urkunden der Ptolemäerzeit* (Berlin, 1922–37), I, 121. E. P. Wegener, also, *Mnemosyne*, 4th series, 1 (1948), 129–130, draws a clear distinction between a judicial appeal and an administrative request.

[17] *Script. Hist. Aug.*, Severus, 9, 5–7; 14, 6. A general amnesty issued by Septimius Severus and Caracalla, now to be ascribed to A.D. 200 instead of 202, is cited by N. Lewis, ΜΕΡΙΣΜΟΣ ΤΩΝ ΑΝΑΚΕΧΟΡΗΚΟΤΩΝ, *JEA*, 23(1937), 66. It is P. Cattaoui II (=Preisigke, *Sammelbuch* I 4284, p. 66).

Lines 8–10

"To Artemidorus, also called Achilles.

"Having placed yourself in agreement with the decisions (rendered), too late you take umbrage at the judgments (given)."

This same decision, in a judicial case, addressed to the same petitioner, Artemidorus with the additional name Achilles, appears in a second copy in P. Amherst 63, lines 4–7. The date of posting in Alexandria is the same in the two copies, namely, Phamenoth 18. The Amherst copy can now be filled out with confidence to read: τοῖς [ἐγνωσμέν]οις συνκαταθέμενος μέμφη τὰ [δόξαντα, πρ]οετέθη, etc. This disposes of the difficulty found in the original reading by the editors of P. Amherst 63. The correction of the impossible μεμφητα to the second person singular μέμφει τά proposed by Ludwig Mitteis can no longer be questioned.[18] There is a reciprocal gain for P. Col. 123 in that the doubtful μέμφη is cleared by the Amherst text.

A second *responsum* of Septimius Severus appears in P. Amherst 63 which was posted upon Phamenoth 24, six days later than the rejection of the request for reconsideration in P. Columbia 123, lines 7–10. It deals with a judicial petition regarding a contract which had become invalid. It was not copied, as not being serviceable, by the person who had the Columbia list of *responsa* transcribed. Ashmunen being the provenience of Amherst papyrus 63, this could mean that this town was *not* the locale at which Columbia papyrus 123 was found.

The suggestion made to us by Professor Leopold Wenger that *tois egnosmenois* serves as the equivalent Greek phrase for the Latin *sententiae*, meaning "decisions rendered," is confirmed by the phrase *tois egnosmenois pithesthai* in line 12 of P. Columbia 123, which means "comply with the decisions given."[19]

Lines 11–12

"To the Aurelii Artemidorus and Anoubion and others.

"Comply with the opinions rendered."

Again there is no indication of the nature of the problem here presented for the emperor's decision. It came from a number of sources. The con-

---

[18] Mitteis, *Grdz.*, No. 376, note, despite Knud Hannestad, *Classica et Mediaevalia*, 6 (1944), 112, note 6.

[19] Compare with Isocrates *Or.* 6. 30 and Demosthenes *Or.* 33.33.

clusion that the inquiry was administrative rather than judicial is based, primarily, upon the observation that several requests had come in upon the same matter; secondarily, upon the meaning of *tois egnosmenois* as explained in the preceding discussion. The cryptic character of the reply leaves the matter in doubt, however.

Lines 13–17

"To Cil-dis, also called Midas, through Philocrates, his son.

"Since you feel decisively that the instrument of sale of the mortgages was unjustly voided, the prefect of the Province will issue the order that you regain possession of the plots seized by force without an agreement."

This is a petition introduced by a son named Philocrates for the revocation of a legal decision against his father. The father, Cil-dis, had held mortgages upon certain plots (*chorion*, line 17) which he had acquired through the nonpayment of loans which he had advanced. These mortgages were of the Greco-Roman type, common in Egypt, of deferred conditional "sales" (*praseis*).[20] When the properties pledged as security were taken over by the lender, Cil-dis, a judgment was given against him in which the document of "sale" was declared invalid and the properties adjudged to the debtor without the consent of the mortgage holder.

The judgment of Septimius Severus is based upon an acceptance of the claim of the petitioner that the "sale" was completely legal and, further, that the return of the mortgaged properties to the debtors in the case was high-handed and done without agreement of the petitioner. The activating of the judgment of the emperor is assigned to the prefect of Egypt, who here again is not mentioned by name and is called "prefect of the province" (*hēgoumenos tou ethnous*, line 17).[21]

Lines 18–20

"To -thalge, daughter of Ambrelus, through her son, Abdomanchus.

"Women are not forbidden to obligate themselves for loans or to exact payment in behalf of others."

Regarding the obviously Semitic character of the names Ambrelus and Abdomanchus, and presumably that of the petitioner -thalge, we have

[20] Rafael Taubenschlag, *Law of Greco-Roman Egypt* (New York, 1944), I 205–206. Characteristic are the documents of the first century after Christ, PSI VIII 908, 910, 911.

[21] Compare p. 23 below and line 51 of the text.

received advice from the following expert Semitists, Professor Ralph Marcus, of the University of Chicago; Professor A. A. Bourham, in conversations at Alexandria University; and notably in a letter dated May 12, 1953, from Professor Adolf Grohmann, of the University of Cairo. The synthesis of their views is that the Greek name *Ambrelos* corresponds to the name 'Amr'il meaning "the servant of God" and found in proto-Arabic inscriptions of Syria and the Sinai peninsula. Professor Grohmann informs me that the name appears, also, in the Greek form *Amr-ilios*, without the phonetic insert of a *beta*. This *beta* insert appears, for example, in the Greek name Ambros, derived from the Arabic.[22] What we have left of the petitioner's name, "-thalge," may well be an Arabic female ending (Grohmann).

Abd-o-manchos, again, is an undoubted Semitic compound with Abd- (servant of), as in Abd-el-malek, "servant of the King." The Greek inter- change of *o* for the Arabic *el-* is frequent (Marcus), as in the name Abd-o- masiamos.[23]

The problem here placed before the emperor was an advisory one. Abdomanchus, of a family of Arabic origin, asked in behalf of his mother regarding the rights of women in financial transactions, more precisely whether they were permitted to pledge themselves for loans and exact pay- ment in behalf of others. Certainly there was doubt in the mind of the petitioner (-thalge) about the situation of women in this respect under the prevailing Egyptian law. The reply clears up the problem in the positive sense that such activities were permissible for women.

The question presented to Severus in this request for direction is in the tradition of the *senatus consultum Velleianum*, usually dated as of A.D. 46. By this decree women who were subject to application of the Roman law were forbidden to act as sureties for any man. The answer of the emperor Severus, applicable to women under the Greco-Roman law of Egypt, is to the effect that women *could* make loans and act in behalf of others in exact- ing payment.[24]

Lines 21–24
"Likewise published in the same Stoa.

[22] See Friedrich Preisigke, *Namenbuch* (Heidelberg, 1922), under the Arabic names, p. 506.
[23] *Ibid.*, p. 505. The scholars who discussed these Arab names have not, as yet, suggested a satisfactory explanation for the last part of the name of the Greek compound, Abd-o-manchos.
[24] An edict of the emperor Claudius had forbidden women to become sureties in matters which involved their husbands, *Cambridge Ancient History*, X, 694 (Charlesworth); Dig. 16. 1. 2. 1: *erat interdictum ne feminae pro viris suis intercederent.*

"To Apollo, son of Harnektotes, and others.

"The (edicts) regarding investigations. A general edict has given consideration to Egyptians."

The laconic form of this answer leaves in doubt the interpretation here presented. There are two factors which cause this indecision despite the preferences presented here in each case. The first is the feminine plural noun which must be understood in line 23 to go with the definite article, *hai*. This seems to me to require the insertion of *kriseis* "the edicts," as an ellipsis of the copyist caused by the repetition of *krisis* in the following phrase, *krisis koine*.

The second difficulty arises from the exact meaning to be given to *episkepseōn* as between its usual significance of inspection of the standing crops in preparation for the land surveys and its less prominent meaning of examinations of evidence for use in court [25] or executive decisions. The translation leaves the decision in doubt by employing the indecisive English word "investigations." The meaning "land inspections" is strongly preferred because of the known number of provincial edicts from Egypt upon an important phase of the agricultural life of the place which can be attributed to its prefects.[26] If there is any provincial edict upon *episkepseis* in the meaning of "proofs" in evidence, differentiated for Alexandrians and Egyptians, it has escaped my observation.

Whether this insertion of *krisis* in line 23 is acceptable or the substitution of some other feminine plural such as the possible *enteuxeis* (petitions) is better, the following *krisis koine* makes a sharp distinction between the

---

[25] In this sense *episkepsis* appears in P. Teb. III 1, 775, 13, an appeal entered by a cleruch for the restoration of his land, in which he asks for an official investigation (*episkepsis*) as to the facts. Cf. P. Teb. III 1, 778, 11, and 797, 28, both of the third century before Christ. For the continuation of the word under the Empire in the meaning of "reports" of the land surveys to be used in evidence see P. Oxy. IX 1188, 27 and 29, and P. Bremen 13, 9, of the early years of the second century after Christ. An Asia Minor inscription, OGI II 502, 9 (A.D. 125–127), mentions the care displayed by the emperors regarding their edicts (*kriseis*). It is also pertinent to observe that Tiberius Julius Alexander in his edict, OGI II 669, 60–66 (translated in A. C. Johnson, *Roman Egypt*, Baltimore, 1936, 708–709), promised that he would write to Rome for the imperial support of the reforms which he was instituting in his provincial edict.

[26] It does not obscure the fact of edictal pronouncements by the prefect that the word for it in the long edict of Tiberius Julius Alexander in A.D. 68 (OGI II 669, 1) is *diatagma*. A clear differentiation between the "divine laws" of the emperor and the provincial edicts (*kriseis*) is made in P. Oxy. VIII 1119, 18, dated A.D. 254. The basic discussion of the provincial edicts upon land inspections is that of M. I. Rostovtzeff, "Studien zur Geschichte des römischen Kolonats," *Archiv für Papyrusforschung, Beiheft* I (1910), in pages 54–147.

provincial edicts, or petitions, as the case may be, and the general edicts emanating from Rome.

In support of the preference for the interpretation of *episkepseis* as land inspections, the long provincial edict of A.D. 68 of the prefect Tiberius Julius Alexander is almost decisive. It makes a sharp distinction in the treatment of the category of the Alexandrians, as a subject class and category and that of the Egyptians respecting the inspections for the surveys and the taxation imposed upon the various qualities of the land. The farms of the Alexandrians within the city jurisdiction and those lying in the Menelaite nome which were attached to the jurisdiction of the city district were not, in the time of Tiberius Alexander as prefect, subject to the annual inspection and the taxes imposed in consequence of it. The "Egyptian" class, however, was subject both to the *episkepsis* and the taxes based upon the subsequent reports.[27]

On the assumption that the two conclusions drawn above in respect to the text are correct, the question put to the emperor and the reply become clear. Multiple requests had come to him, from a certain Apollo and from other local administrators, citing edicts of previous prefects on the subject of the position of the "Egyptians" as they were affected by the inspections of their farm holdings and the subsequent taxation on their produce as determined by the categories of "inundated," "unflooded," "dry" land, or land subject to tax reductions (*hypologos gē*). How were the rules to be applied in the case of the *Aigyptioi*? The answer of the emperor is that their status in this respect had been covered in a general edict. Whether this was an imperial pronouncement of Septimius Severus himself or of one of his predecessors remains uncertain.

Lines 25–27

"To Aurelius Sarapion.

"Some time ago we forbade that inheritances from the mother's side should come down in succession."

The first word, *proen*, in the general significance of "formerly" or "some time ago" is fully attested by the early Empire documents P. Amherst 66, line 39, as shown by the *kai proteron* of line 37, by P. Tebtunis II 286, line 4 (Hadrian); and by Corpus Pap. Raineri I 19, line 3, of A.D. 330. For later examples consult Preisigke, *WB*, s.v.

[27] OGI II 669, sections 12–15, lines 55–65.

The question, strictly a legal one, was presented by a petitioner who was interested in the problem of the succession to property left by cognates in the mother's line. The *responsum* is negative and based upon a previous decision, apparently rendered by Septimius Severus himself (*ekolusamen*, "we forbade").

Lines 28–34
"To Proclus, son of Apollonius.

"It is not just that the heirs written in wills—the wills may even be said to have given rise (to them as heirs)—have been ejected from their right of possession. Those who have introduced the cases will take care to summon those who are being charged, if, indeed, the affair is of the type of case requiring jurisdiction requiring a special judge."

This is the response to an inquiry regarding the rights of persons named as legatees in a will. Its explanation here offered was greatly furthered by the observation of Professor Leopold Wenger that the clause is a parenthetical one which reads: "the wills may even be said to have given rise (to them)."

This parenthetical clause is a statement of principle, that the presence of names in a will raises a primary presumption that the persons so named were legally entitled to acceptance as legatees. Their rights cannot be disregarded summarily. The applicant for judicial advice in this case, acting in behalf of heirs named in a will, is told what the petitioners whom he is representing are to do in the event that the case is of the *diagnosis*, or special judge, type.

Lines 35–39
"To Cronius, son of Heraclides.

"Transient sicknesses do not afford relief from municipal liturgies. Those who are physically sick are subject to liturgical services if they are mentally capable of conducting their household affairs."

The demands for exemptions from the liturgical services which begin to appear so markedly in the first half of the second century reached a high point in the Principate of Septimius Severus. In one papyrus in the Florence collection, for example, there are six different rescripts upon the matter to be ascribed to Severus emanating from the period of his stay in Egypt.[28]

[28] P. Flor. 382. Ulrich Wilcken, *Archiv für Papyrusforschung*, IV (1908), 435, 437; Wilcken' *Grdz.*, 344. The dates retained in P. Flor. 57 (= III 382), even where the condition of the papyrus leaves the meaning in doubt, are important for the chronology of the stay of Severus in Egypt.

The first of these, dated December 17 (Hadrianus 21), A.D. 199, established the old-age exemption date at the seventieth birthday.

The request for administrative information which lies behind this reply of Severus is in regard to exemption from the customary state services because of sickness. The answer is as clear as it is rigid. Passing physical sicknesses are not to be accepted as excuses sufficient to release the applicant from a liturgy.[29] The only valid reason here permitted is mental incapacity so severe that the sufferer cannot conduct his own household affairs.[30]

The idea adverbially expressed in the phrase "physically sick" (literally, weak in body) makes it clear that an official distinction was made in the types of incapacity included under the term "weak persons" (astheneis). This supports the preference of Friedrich Oertel in some cases for understanding as economic rather than therapeutic some of the "weaknesses" presented in requests for exemptions from liturgical services.[31]

Lines 40–44

"Likewise (i.e., also posted in the Stoa).

"To Dioscorus, son of Hephaestion, and to Piesis, son of Osiris, and others.

"We have forbidden that you pay money in place of grain."

The Egyptian name Piesis, here meaning "the man of Iris," is already known from the second and third centuries after Christ, both as masculine and as feminine appellation.[32]

The question here put before the emperor had come from a number of different private sources. They asked about the permissibility of paying money in lieu of tax payments customarily required in grain. The possibility that obligations existing between private persons are here concerned is excluded because, as between them, the nature of the payment would have been determined by private negotiation, and the response would not be couched in terms of "we have forbidden you." The question is, therefore, one of conversion of grain payments into corresponding equivalents in coinage. The *adaeration* is forbidden by the emperor, and the refusal is based upon

---

[29] By implication this would mean that chronic diseases, *chronioi nosoi* in the Hippocratic vocabulary, might be considered in applications for exemption.

[30] In a will of the time of Trajan the phrase used in Egypt for freedom from mental illnesses is "being in sound health and in control over myself," ὑγιαίνοντι ὑπὲρ ἐμαυτοῦ, BGU VII 1654, 5–6.

[31] Friedrich Oertel, *Die Liturgie* (Leipzig, 1917), p. 390, note 5.

[32] Preisigke, *Namenbuch*, s.v. Πεῆσις.

some previous decision, possibly of Septimius himself, which did not permit it.[33]

Lines 45–51

"To Isidorus, son of Dius.

"His Excellency, Fulvius Plautianus, prefect of the camps and our household companion, will conduct the investigation of the audacious actions (emanating) from Comon. In respect to Apion, the tax collector, if he is not involved with Comon in the charges (against him, Comon) you will have the prefect of the province as judge."

The appellant, Isidorus, presented an accusation against two officials, a higher-placed one named Comon and a tax collector named Apion. Since the more serious accusation against Comon was assigned for investigation to the praetorian prefect, Fulvius Plautianus,[34] it is a possibility that Comon occupied a position as high as that of a strategus of the nome of residence of the appellant, Isidorus. The imperial decision has two parts: the designation of court, or courts, to which the case is to be assigned, and the suggestion that the action may have to be divided against the two accused officials, Comon and Apion. In the event that the charges against Apion were not clearly involved in those against Comon, the affair should be divided. In the accusation against Comon, the praetorian prefect would be delegated as judge; and the lesser case, that against Apion, would be assigned to the prefect of Egypt.[35]

Lines 52–56

"To Isidorus, also called Heraclides, through Apollonius.

"Although you gave a deed of cession in the matter of your paternal inheritance and do not have the assistance (arising) from minority status, you assert that, under the law of sales, confiscation has been applied against the estate. Comply."

The petitioner was evidently a young man, just over the threshold of

[33] The historical setting and importance of this *apokrima* will be presented more fully in the following section.

[34] Brief sketches of the career of C. Fulvius Plautianus are to be found in the study of Laurence L. Howe, *The Pretorian Prefects from Commodus to Diocletian* (Chicago, 1947), pp. 69–70, and in Stein, *Die Präfekten von Ägypten*, pp. 110–111.

[35] The use of the title ὁ ἡγούμενος τοῦ ἔθνους for the prefect of Egypt, with particular reference to *ethnos* as "province," has been discussed above, p. 13, in the section upon the question of the borrowing of Latin legal terms.

legal maturity. By a *syngraphe apostasiou* (Latin, *bonorum cessio*) he had renounced claim to an inheritance from his father. Later he raised the objection, as mentioned in the response to his appeal, that his property had been confiscated. The decision of the emperor was that his claim for reversal of the previous judgment was unfounded. The denial of his appeal rests upon the technical point that he was no longer in a position, because of his age, to ask for the assistance granted by law to persons of immature years. This assistance he apparently had invoked.

The legal protections of youth and those granting exemptions from liturgical burdens because of old age and mental sickness, the latter as indicated in this list of petitions in lines 35–39, were being strictly adhered to by the emperor. In P. Oxyrhynchus VII 1020 two additional *responsa* of Septimius Severus cite the assistance granted to those under legal age. In both cases the locale of the publication of the decisions is given as Alexandria, but their dates are lost. In both cases the investigation into the age of the appellant is assigned to the prefect of Egypt, designated as in line 51 of our document, as the "ruler of the province" (*hegoumenos tou ethnous*). In the first of the two cases in P. Oxyrhynchus 1020 the appellant was a minor, or just over the age of legal majority, who had requested, because of his minority status, release from some burden imposed upon him. The second case was that of a girl, represented in her petition by a freedman. The freedman, who acted as her legal representative, alleged that fraud (*apate*) had been used in the previous conduct of the case.

Lines 57–60

"To -elatheus, son of Caerenus.

"If you take guardians for orphans outside of the (regular) order, in respect to their properties a judge of special delegation will be given against those assigned (i.e., against the guardians)."

The request in this case was one for guidance, presented by a magistrate who had the appointment of guardians as a part of his official duties and the obligation of presenting the cases against the guardians if irregularities occurred in their handling of the properties of their wards. The appointing official wished to know what his procedure would be in case he selected guardians for orphaned children outside of some order which was legally recommended. The answer is clear. In such cases, if any irregularities appeared on the part of the guardians their trials would come before a court of special appointment.   This implies that the regular courts would act if the guardians had been appointed in the recommended order.

An important feature of this *responsum* lies in the assurance which it brings that a conclusion drawn by Rafael Taubenschlag regarding the assignment of guardians in Egypt is confirmed: "Statutory guardianship of wards," says Taubenschlag, "was known in peregrine law and both paternal and maternal cognates were called upon in a certain order of procedure." [36] The statutory provision upon this point must have been permissive rather than mandatory.

[36] Rafael Taubenschlag, *Law of Greco-Roman Egypt*, I, 120, and note 15.

HISTORICAL IMPLICATIONS OF
P. COLUMBIA 123 REGARDING THE STAY
OF SEVERUS IN EGYPT

THE CHIEF IMPORTANCE of the Columbia *apokrimata* of the Emperor Severus lies, of course, in what his decisions may add to the knowledge of Roman law and the peregrine law of Egypt at the time of his visit. This is the specialist's task. Secondarily, but not without significance, it brings details of considerable historical interest. Among these is the archeological fact of the presence of a Stoa in the Gymnasium at Alexandria which was prominently used in the time of Severus as a place of publication for edicts.[37] For the chronology of the visit of Septimius Severus in Egypt in his eighth year by the local Egyptian reckoning it adds certain dates, fixed to the day or month. That this visit occurred in A.D. 199–200 rather than in A.D. 202 was established over thirty years ago and has been generally accepted by interested scholars since that time.[38]

For the convenience of future workers in the field of the judicial and administrative activity of the period, lists are here set up of the known *apokrimata* of the emperor Severus as they appear in the papyri. The first group, (A) of list I, presents those constitutions of the emperor in which the dates of publication appear. The second group contains those from which the dates have been lost or into which they were not inserted.

[37] W. L. Westermann, "Alexandria in the Greek Papyri," *Bulletin de la Société Royale d'Archeologie d'Alexandrie*, No. 38 (1949), p. 11. The Stoa of the Gymnasium was probably a different one from that built in A.D. 205 at the behest of Severus. See Aristide Calderini, *Dizionario di nomi geografici e topografici dell' Egitto* (Cairo, 1935), I, 1, s.v. *Alexandria*.

[38] It was fixed by Hasebroek in his *Untersuchungen zur Geschichte des Kaisers Septimius Severus*, p. 122. Consult, also, E. P. Wegener, *Symbolae von Oven* (Leiden, 1946), p. 161, and Hannestad, *Classica et Mediaevalia*, 6 (1944), p. 195.

LIST I (A). DECISIONS OF SEPTIMIUS SEVERUS
WITH DATES OF PUBLICATION

1. P. Flor. III 382, 17–32. December 18 (Hadrianus 27) of A.D. 199(?).[39]
2. P. Flor. III 382, 24–26. Dec. 18 (Hadrianus 27), A.D. 199(?).
3. BGU I 267, 14. Dec. 29 (Tybi 3), A.D. 199; and a second copy of this, P. Strass. 22, 9 (Mitteis, *Chrest.* 374, dated April 19 (Pharmouthi 24), A.D. 200.
4. P. Flor. 382, 1–4. February 22 (Mecheir 26), A.D. 200.
5. P. Amh. 63, 1–6. March 14 (Phamenoth 18), A.D. 200. This *responsum* is repeated, as having been posted in the Stoa of the Alexandrian Gymnasium, with the same dates, year, month, and day, in our document, P. Col. 123, 8–10.
6–17. P. Col. 123. March 14 (Phamenoth 18), A.D. 200.[40]
18. P. Amh. 63, 7–12. March 20 (Phamenoth 24), A.D. 200.
19. BGU II 473, 12. Late March-April (Pharmouthi, day lost), A.D. 200.
20. P. Oxy. XII 1405, 12–13. Late March-April (Pharmouthi, day not entered), A.D. 200.

LIST I (B). DECISIONS OF SEVERUS IN EGYPT
IN YEAR 8 (A.D. 199–200), IN WHICH DATES ARE LOST

21. P. Flor. III 382, 10–12.
22. P. Flor. III 382, 13–16.
23. P. Flor. III 382, 27–46.
24. P. Oxy. VII 1020, 1–6.
25. P. Oxy. VII 1020, 7–8.
26. P. London, Inv. 2565, published by T. C. Skeat and E. P. Wegener, *JEA*, XXI (1935), 229–233, lines 105–106.
27. P. Oxy. IV 705, 35–39. Late in A.D. 199 or early in 200.
28. P. Aber. 15. Right half of edict or rescript.
    To this list we add three more documents issued by Severus, with the added name of Caracalla, which are not technically *responsa*.
29. The first is an edict, of A.D. 199–200, bidding the Egyptians residing in foreign places and those who were making trouble within Egypt to return to their places of origin and to cease from violence. This is P.

[39] Upon this badly broken document, consult Wilcken, *Archiv für Papyrusforschung*, VI (1908), 437–443.
[40] These twelve do not include P. Col. 123, 8–10, which is a repetition of No. 5 above, P. Amh. 63, 1–6.

Cattaoui II, lines 6–8, published by Léon Barry in *Bulletin de l' Institut d' Archéologie Orientale du Caire*, III (1903), 187–202, and reproduced in Friedrich Preisigke, *Sammelbuch* (Strassburg, 1915–50), I as No. 4284.[41]

30. P. Oxy. VI 899, *verso*, 18–21, described upon p. 226. Badly splattered, but containing clearly the words: "Emperor Caesar Lucius Septim(ius) Severus Pius" and the date, "year 8, Pharmouthi 18." Apparently an edict.

31. P. Berlin Inv. 7346, *verso*, 19–20, three fragments published by H. Frisk, *Aegyptus*, IX (1928), 281–284, cf. Preisigke, *Sammelbuch* IV 7366 and Taubenschlag, *JJP*, VI (1952), 130, No. 13. Line 50 gives the date and diplomatics type as "Decision of our Lords, year 8, Phamenoth 8 (=March 4, A.D. 200)."

LIST II. CONTENT OF THE DECISIONS OF SEVERUS
(WITH ADDED NAME OF CARACALLA)

1. P. Flor. III 382, 17–23. Content unclear.
2. P. Flor. III 382, 24–26. Content unclear.
3. BGU I 267, 14, and P. Strass. 22. Regarding uncontested possession of property lasting over a long period.
4. P. Flor. 382, 1–4. Release from liturgies at seventy years.
5. P. Amh. 63, 1–6. } Rejection of an appeal upon technical grounds.
   P. Col. 123, 8–10. }
6. P. Col. 123, 5–7. Remission of fines imposed upon Alexandrians and the class of "Egyptians."
7. P. Col. 123, 11–12. Subject unclear. Administrative order to follow previous decisions.
8. P. Col. 123, 13–17. Appeal regarding illegal seizure. Rehearing granted.
9. P. Col. 123, 18–20. Women permitted to borrow and to exact payment for others.
10. P. Col. 123, 22–24. Reference to a previous general edict upon "investigations," presumably meaning reports upon crops, in which the class of "Egyptians" had been covered.
11. P. Col. 123, 25–27. Question regarding inheritances from the mother's side. A former decision forbade it.

[41] Line 6: "when they rose [like the sun] in Egypt."

12. P. Col. 123, 28–34. Question regarding rights of heirs named in a will. Principle that they cannot be summarily dispossessed.

13. P. Col. 123, 35–39. Administrative inquiry as to relief from liturgies because of sickness. Response—only complete mental disability warrants exemption.

14. P. Col. 123, 41–44. Administrative problem. Payment of money in lieu of grain payments is forbidden.

15. P. Col. 123, 45–51. Question regarding disposition of a case of official malfeasance. The case may be divisible, one part to come before the praetorian prefect, the other before the provincial prefect.

16. P. Col. 123, 52–56. Judicial appeal regarding an inheritance case. Previous decision upheld.

17. P. Col. 123, 57–60. Question upon court of reference in a case of guardianship of orphans. Referred to a court of special delegation.

18. P. Amh. 63, 7–12. (Badly shattered.) A settlement by *dialysis* (agreement out of court) is mentioned.

19. BGU II 473, 12. Deals with a resignation of property (*cessio bonorum*), presumably to avoid taking office.

20. P. Oxy. XII 1905. Resignation of property to escape liturgical office holding. It does not impair citizenship or bring liability to corporal punishment.

21. P. Flor. III, 10–12. Immunity from liturgies at age seventy.

22. P. Flor. III 382, 13–16. Again—freedom from liturgies at age seventy.

23. P. Flor. III 382, 27–46. Petition for relief from liturgy at age seventy.

24. P. Oxy. VII 1020, 5–6. Request for release from some unspecified obligation. Referred to the prefect of Egypt.

25. P. Oxy. VII 1020, 7–8. Complaint of a young woman about deceitful practice. If she is a minor, case referred to the prefect of Egypt.

26. P. London inv. 2565, 52–84 and 105–106. (Skeat and Wegener, *JEA*, XXI [1905], 229–233). Forbids enlistment of villagers for metropolitan liturgies.

27. P. Oxy. IV 705, 64–74. Request for permission to establish a foundation to assist villagers to carry on liturgies. Permission granted, lines 54–63.

28. P. Aberdeen 15. Right half only. Edict or rescript about painters. Three additional constitutions of the two emperors which are not *responsa* (*apokrimata*).

29. P. Cattaoui II 6–8, *Bulletin de l' Institut d'Archaéologie Orientale du Caire*, 3 (1903), 127–200; Preisigke, *Sammelbuch* I 4284. Imperial edict [42] ordering Egyptians to return to their towns or other places of origin.

30. P. Oxy. VI 899, *verso*, 18–21. Apparently an edict, exempting women from undertaking production upon imperial domains.

31. P. Berlin Inv. 7346, *verso*, 19–20. Frisk, *Aegyptus*, IX (1928), 281–284. Grant of a privilege. Content unclear.

The lists above offer an impressive body of administrative and judicial activities of the emperor Severus and his advisers during the year of his sojourn in Egypt. The twenty *apokrimata* which have retained their dates fix the span of the period of these decisions, rendered at Alexandria, certainly as extending from December 18, A.D. 199, into the month Pharmouthi, March 27–April 25, of A.D. 200.[43] They leave not the slightest remaining doubt that the stay of Septimius in Egypt occurred in his eighth year, 199–200, as against the older reference of it to A.D. 202. It is still advisable to hold to the general dating of his arrival there, advanced some thirty years ago by Johannes Hasebroek, namely, November of A.D. 199,[44] rather than to follow the close reasoning of Knud Hannestad which would place the entry into Egypt before August 29 of A.D. 199.[45]

In 1917 J. G. Milne suggested that the granting to Alexandria and the *metropoleis* in Egypt of the right to have their own metropolitan senates (*boulai*) should be put back by two years from the then accepted date of A.D. 202 to A.D. 200.[46] The idea was entertained by Johannes Hasebroek in 1921 and accepted by Ulrich Wilcken because of his acquaintance with the increasing knowledge of the activity of Severus in Egypt in the earlier year.[47]

[42] An edict of the Prefect of Egypt, Sabatianus Aquila, reinforcing this order, is mentioned in P. Geneva 16, 18–21, dated October 11, A.D. 207. See U. Wilcken, *Chrest.* No. 354.

[43] The last entry of the dated list (I (A) above, No. 20, P. Oxy. XII 1405, 12–13) reads: "Posted in Alexandria, year 8, Pharmouthi." The list here prepared should be checked with the document of year 8 of Septimius collected by Aristide Calderini in *Aegyptus*, XX (1940), 330–331, and with Rafael Taubenschlag's useful organization of "Imperial Constitutions in the Papyri," *JJP*, VI (1952), 121–142.

[44] Hasebroek, *Untersuchungen zur Geschichte des Kaiser Septimius Severus*, pp. 116–122.

[45] Hannestad, *Classica et Mediaevalia*, 6 (1944), 202–207. The author works from a probability of a festive entry into Alexandria, based upon numismatic evidence (pp. 204–205), and draws from this a "necessary consequence." The minting of a commemorative coin may, however, be anticipatory.

[46] J. G. Milne, "Some Alexandrian Coins," *JEA*, IV (1917), 180, and note 1.

[47] Hasebroek, *Untersuchungen zur Geschichte des Kaisers Septimius Severus*, p. 123; Wilcken, *Archiv für Papyrusforschung*, VII (1924), 85.

The suggestion gained in solidity through the publication in 1934 of an Oxyrhynchus papyrus which informs us of a man who was a local senator in Alexandria in May-June of A.D. 201.[48] Since Milne's suggestion in 1917 the new dating of the founding of the metropolitan senates in Egypt has been receiving more constant support.[49]

As Hasebroek declared, the grant of a local senate to the city of Alexandria cannot well be looked upon as an isolated event. It is inherently probable that the institution of the local senates in the nome capitals in Egypt should be associated with that event. The number of the *responsa* issued by Severus in Egypt in year 8 is now so great that the year 199–200 as that of his visit cannot be doubted. Spartianus placed his trip into Egypt after the Parthian campaign of A.D. 199 and after the stop in Syria and Palestine.[50] In the following year he set the granting of the local senate to the Alexandrians.[51]

It is true that in the total number of the advisory and judicial replies of Severus which we have there is no specific support for the date A.D. 200 as that of the establishment of the local senates in the Egyptian *metropoleis*. It is the total group of them which leaves the strong impression that a momentous innovation had occurred which had bewildered the local officials of that province and had produced the unusual stream of requests for enlightenment. Noticeable in List II above is the number of the questions and replies of the emperor which deal with problems of the liturgies. There are three which have to do with matters of inheritances (numbers 11, 12, and 16 of List II) and again three which raise problems concerning the protection of minors (numbers 17, 23, and 24). In contrast with these groups of three there are nine replies which have to do with matters arising from the liturgical system. This number suggests a radical reorganization of the former requirements for the holding of compulsory offices (the *archai*) and of the other compulsory state services which comprised the liturgies. Women who had inherited fortunes sufficient to place their possessors in the category of those subject to appointment to a magistracy could not serve as liturgists. In lieu

[48] Gabriella Schöpflech, *Studi italiani di filologia classica*, n.s., XII (1935), 105–108, line 3.

[49] J. G. Milne, *History of Egypt under Roman Rule* (London, 1924), p. 141; Oscar W. Reinmuth, *The Prefect of Egypt, Klio, Beiheft*, 34, No. 5, No. 31 (1935), 55; A. H. M. Jones, *Cities of the Eastern Roman Provinces*, (Oxford, 1937), p. 329. E. P. Wegener, "The βουλαί of the Metropoleis," in *Symbolae van Oven* (Leiden, 1946), pp. 161–162; S. N. Miller, in *Cambridge Ancient History*, XII, 18.

[50] Hasebroek, *Untersuchungen zur Geschichte des Kaisers Septimius Severus*, p. 123.

[51] *Script. Hist. Aug.* Severus, 16–17: *post hoc dato stipendio cumulatiore militibus Alexandriam petit. . . . Deinde Alexandrinis jus bulutarum dedit. . . . Multa praeterea his jura mutavit.*

thereof they were compelled to pay an appointment tax, *stephanikon archonton*. This is known from an account as yet unpublished, as far as is known to me. It is dated A.D. 198, the year preceding the entry of Severus into Egypt.[52] This is an extension of the financial demands upon the well-to-do in Egypt which is probably to be ascribed to Severus. In addition to this Miss Wegener has elsewhere suggested that the practice of resignation of one's property (*cessio bonorum*) in order to escape the burden of compulsory office-holding or other liturgies seems to have been introduced into Egypt by Severus.[53] This new evidence upon the activities of Severus while in Egypt strengthens the growing conviction that the changes which he then set in motion were both fundamental in character and far-reaching in their detailed application. The latter point was clearly stated by Spartianus: "Besides this he changed many laws for them (the Egyptians)." [54]

The *responsum* in lines 41–44 of Columbia papyrus 123 reads: "We have forbidden that you pay money in place of grain." The question which it answers, as it has been interpreted above, came in from several tax payers. They wished to know whether taxes regularly deliverable in wheat might be met with equated money payments. The adverse decision, emanating from the emperor's official group, is based upon a previous decision—"we have forbidden (*ekolusamen*)"—possibly a general edict applying to the entire Empire. Whether local to Egypt or general in its application, it must be considered in connection with the information furnished by Spartianus that when Severus died he left a surplus of grain large enough to meet for seven years the requirements, presumably of Rome, permitting the distribution of 75,000 pecks per day. The amount of oil which he left behind was sufficient to meet the needs of the city and of Italy as well when necessary, for a five-year period.[55]

This answer to numerous inquiries must also be placed in its setting in

[52] Information sent by Sir Harold Bell to Miss E. P. Wegener, *Symbolae van Oven*, pp. 175 (note 3), 176.

[53] E. P. Wegener, "The βουλή and the Nomination to the ἀρχαί," *Mnemosyne*, 4th Series, I (1948), 119–120. With remarkable prevision M. I. Rostovtzeff sketched the policy of Septimius Severus in Egypt with respect to the separation of the municipal liturgies and the state burdens which were to rest upon the peasants. See his *Social and Economic History of the Roman Empire* (Oxford, 1926), p. 360.

[54] *Script. Hist. Aug.*, Severus, 17, 3: *multa praeterea his jura mutavit.*

[55] Spartianus, *Script. Hist. Aug.*, Severus, 23, 2; cf. 8, 5; 18, 2; and Aelius Lampridius, *ibid.*, Severus Alexander, 22, 2. Rostovtzeff, in the early years of his career, postulated an important change in the system of grain distribution which began under Severus. It appeared in his study of the Roman lead tokens, *Römische Bleitesserae*, *Klio*, Supplement III (Leipzig, 1905), p. 18.

the financial policy of the Principate of Septimius Severus. We have some knowledge of a coinage issue by him in which the silver content of the imperial coins was reduced from 74.7 per cent to 52.8 per cent.[56] It is not possible to connect the decision of P. Columbia 123, lines 43–44, directly with the new issue by Severus because of lack of knowledge of the year of that event; but the numismatic finds in Egypt have brought proof that the Roman denarius circulated there in the reign of Severus as never before that time.[57] The wide use of the debased denarius may help to explain the desire of the Egyptian tax payers to meet their government obligations in coinage rather than in grain, if permissible.

The refusal of the government to allow the *adaeration* becomes understandable if the imperial denarius was already in circulation in Egypt in A.D. 200. From the administrative point of view the *adaeration* into money payments which they, the renters and tax payers, desired, would have been to the advantage of those taxed and the tenants of the large and small holdings of the imperial domain.[58] If, on the other hand, the government could maintain the fictitious value which it had set upon its silver currency, at a rate higher than its acceptance value in the open market, the financial advantage to the administration of its insistence upon payments *in natura* would be obvious.[59] The advantages would lie with the government: the disadvantages would rest upon the tenants of government domains and the tax payers. The effect of the inflation can be seen as it showed itself in Severus's time in Caria in one of the last two years of his reign. There it brought in its train the usual "black marketeering" and currency speculation which the

---

[56] See the tables of the imperial and the Alexandrian coinage set up by Gunnar Mickwitz, *Geld und Wirtschaft im römischen Reich des IV Jahrhunderts* (Helsingfors, 1932), p. 40. The decline in the silver content was put at 30 per cent by Fluss, "Severus (13)," *RE*, 2, 1897. Cf. the remarks of Fritz Heichelheim on the effects upon the acceptance of Roman coinage outside of the empire, *Wirtschaftsgeschichte des Altertums* (Leiden, 1938), I, 685.

[57] Dattari in *Rivista italiana numismatica* (1903), pp. 285–286. For the restriction of the output of the local Alexandrian mint and its coinage during the period of rule of Septimius Severus and Caracalla, consult J. G. Milne, "Some Alexandrian Coins," *JEA*, IV (1917), 181.

[58] See Mickwitz, *Geld und Wirtschaft*, pp. 121–122, 166, for the insistence of the Swedish government in the eighteenth century upon tax payments in kind and the attitude of the grain growers toward it. Note, also, the comprehensive analysis on p. 190. Aristide Calderini, *I Severi; la crisi del impero nel III secolo* (Bologna, 1949), pp. 370, 378, has dealt briefly with the consequences of the inflation of the time.

[59] For the wish of the producers to shift from money payments to payments *in natura* according to their advantage under differing conditions see Otto Seeck, "*Adaeratio*," in Pauly-Wissowa-Kroll, *RE*, 1, 840–841.

local authorities tried to check by the imposition of fines upon the free and beatings and imprisonment upon slaves.[60]

In the analysis of the rule of Septimius Severus it must be remembered that the financial situation which he faced when he became emperor was not of his contriving. The minting of coinage of like weight but lowered silver content had already begun to take on serious proportions in the first half of the second century after Christ.[61] It is true that the financial outlook had worsened during the first six years of Severus's Principate through the succession struggles and the Parthian war. The list of his administrative and judicial replies to inquiries during his stay in Egypt seems to offer the opportunity for a reappraisal of his activities during the last twelve years of his career. As viewed within the frame of his period and its inexorable financial deterioration [62] the new information regarding the decisions which he made in Egypt will not lessen his stature or diminish the scope of his efforts. Surely the judgment that Septimius Severus "was a typical product of the second century, a Roman bureaucrat," [63] will not be strengthened by the study of the *responsa* now available in the papyri.

[60] Wilhelm Dittenberger, *Orientis Graeci Inscriptiones* II, 525; David Magie, *Roman Rule in Asia Minor* (Princeton, N.J., 1950), I, 681–682.

[61] Mickwitz, *Geld und Wirtschaft*, pp. 32–50.

[62] For the frustration of the efforts of Septimius Severus to meet the financial crisis of his time and the ruination of the middle class through the attempts which he made to establish a firm base for his taxation system, see Roger Remondon's study, "Ἀπορικόν et Μερισμὸς Ἀπόρων," *Annales du Service des Antiquités de l'Égypte*, 51 (1951), 221–245, with especial reference to Severus on pages 224–245.

[63] This view of Severus was expressed by Mason Hammond, "Septimius Severus, Roman Bureaucrat," *Harvard Studies in Classical Philology*, LI (1940), 167 and 172. This estimate was based upon a study of his activities which considered only the early years of Septimius's career, to A.D. 193.   The inclusion of the activities of the last twelve years of his life, beginning with the Egyptian visit which produced the *apokrimata* which we have assembled, will certainly alter this characterization. Septimius might, in his early years, be correctly called a typical career politician of the second century, but not a "bureaucrat," as head of a bureau.

APOKRIMATA
LEGAL COMMENTARY
by A. Arthur Schiller

PRELIMINARY NOTE

THE LEGAL COMMENT to the Columbia papyrus (P. Columbia 123) comprises a discussion of the individual texts which have collectively been termed *apokrimata* by the scribe, and a treatment of legal problems directly raised by the opening lines or heading. Each of the thirteen texts concerns a distinct topic, while in totality they run the gamut of civil, criminal, and administrative law and reflect the various legal systems simultaneously in effect in Egypt at the beginning of the third century of our era. The single papyrus might thus have afforded a point of departure for a comprehensive evaluation of the status of law in Egypt in all its manifold aspects in the years immediately preceding the *constitutio Antoniniana*. Or it might have served as the starting point for a discussion of the impact of imperial legal activity in the province, more specifically, of the juridical significance of the visit of the emperor Septimius Severus, with the young Caracalla, to Egypt.

In the view of the writer, however, comment on a single papyrus is preferably limited to the content of the document itself. In the case of the Columbia *apokrimata* papyrus this means a discussion of those of the thirteen "decisions" which provide information sufficient for an exposition of their legal significance. One cannot be dogmatic about the nature of any of these terse replies. It is the task of the commentator to weigh the probabilities and develop the hypothesis he deems will be in best accord with the information provided. It must be remembered that there are always a number of possible inferences. Consequently, no attempt has been made to reconcile views expressed in the two parts of this volume. Indeed, the reader may even hazard another view as more plausible than any presented. Only with the edition of similar texts, should they exist, and with deeper study of comparable published papyri, will the meaning of each of the "decisions" be more definitely determined. The opening lines of the Columbia papyrus clearly raise two topics for discussion, namely, the method by which these "decisions" were made known and the language in which these replies were drafted. The conclusions reached in the comment reveal that P. Columbia 123 confirms the presently accepted views on those subjects. A third topic, the purpose for which the papyrus was written, affords a theme for a conclusion to the comment.

To Professor Westermann the writer is most sincerely indebted for the kindness and encouragement given during their many years as colleagues in Columbia University, dating back to the time when as a student he was first introduced into the field of papyrological studies by one already recognized as a master. It is particularly gratifying to be able to express these thanks in this joint effort on the occasion of the bicentennial celebration of the university we both have served. Thanks are due to Professor Ernst Levy and to the late Professor Leopold Wenger for suggestions each of them made upon brief but penetrating contact with a preliminary reading of the papyrus. Professor Adolf Berger has been most gracious in offering his extraordinary knowledge of the law of the Roman world, papyrological as well as classical Roman and Byzantine. The views expressed in this comment, however, are those of the author and he takes full responsibility for them.

The author is also indebted to scores of papyrological works, editions of primary sources as well as secondary discussion in books and articles. Sources and literature of the Roman law were also extensively utilized. Annotation to these materials is at a minimum for reference to further literature on specific texts is provided in the introductions to the papyri republished in *Leges* or *Negotia*, while supplementary secondary literature is noted in the standard works of Professors Taubenschlag, Wenger, and Berger. These as well as other major works and periodicals are listed in the Table of Abbreviations; the other abbreviations employed are those familiar in papyrological and legal publications.

The primary basis of comment of any papyrus are the words of the papyrus itself. Lexical studies were of necessity the fundamental first steps in the preparation of legal comment. Use was made of the recognized Greek dictionaries, word-lists of Greek authors, and the specialized works of Preisigke as well as the indices of the most significant collections of published papyri of recent years. For possible Latin equivalents Professor Berger's excellent Encyclopedic Dictionary and the well-known specialized vocabularies of Latin legal sources have proven of inestimable value. Bilingual Greek and Latin glosses and texts have been canvassed. It has not been considered necessary to indicate in notes the precise references to the scores of words thus analyzed. The specialist is familiar with the method followed and can easily verify the meanings assigned, and he would only be disturbed by a plethora of annotations if each such lexical conclusion were attested.

HEADING

ΕΝ ΑΛΕΞΑΝΔΡΕΙΑ

1-4   αντιγραφα αποκριματων τεθεντων εν τη στοα
του γυμνασιου. η (ετους) Φαμενωθ ιη. Αυτοκρατωρ Καισαρ Λουκιος
Σεπ]τιμιος Σηουηρος Ευσεβης Περτιναξ Αραβικος Αδιαβηνικος Παρθικος Μεγιστος
Σεβαστος και Αυτοκρατωρ Καισαρ Μαρκος Αυρηλιος Αντωνεινος Σεβαστος.

21   κ[αι] ομοιως προετεθη εν τη αυτη στοα.

40   Κ(αι) ομοιως.

> In Alexandria. Copies of decisions posted in the stoa of
> the Gymnasium, year 8, Phamenoth 18. Imperator Caesar
> Lucius Septimius Severus Pius Pertinax Arabicus Adiabenicus
> Parthicus Maximus Augustus and Imperator Caesar Marcus
> Aurelius Antoninus Augustus.
> Likewise posted in the same stoa.
> Likewise.

The "decisions" (apokr'mata) which have been copied from the stoa of the Gymnasium in Alexandria are actually examples of that type of enactment of the emperor technically known as subscript (subscriptio, hypographē), a form of rescript. It seems of first order, therefore, to demonstrate why these texts are subscripts and in what fashion they came to be called decisions.

THE POSTING OF RESCRIPTS

Professor Ulrich Wilcken, the master of papyrological studies, published an article in 1920 describing the manner in which rescripts of the emperor were made known to the recipients of these imperial pronouncements.[1] It had long been recognized that two distinct types of this form of *constitutio* had been employed from Hadrian's time on. Questions directed to the emperor from private persons or from public officials were answered either by

---

[1] "Zu den Kaiserreskripten," *Hermes*, 55 (1920), 1–42.

letter or by subscript attached to the petition itself. Further, it was known that answers to officials were regularly made by letter, while private persons were answered by subscripts. Some of the rescripts reproduced in the legal sources employed a purely epistolary form. Others in the legal sources and preserved in inscriptions were noted as signed (scripsi) and posted (proposita). There were differences of opinion regarding the posting. Professor Karlowa, for example, believed that publication of rescripts was for the purpose of bringing the authoritative answers of the emperor to the attention of the people.[2] Dr. Mommsen, on the other hand, thought that only those rescripts destined to have the force of law were posted, though he admitted that others might be published in Rome to permit them to be read by all those interested.[3] Professor Krüger wondered how this idea was to be reconciled with the posting of imperial rescripts in Alexandria, as some of the published papyri had shown they had been.[4]

Professor Wilcken put all of these uncertainties to rest. Through a brilliant analysis of papyrological and inscriptional sources he proved that not only were there two distinct forms of rescript but there was a regular procedure for handling each of the two types, procedures which remained fairly constant from Hadrian to the time of Justinian. The petitions from officials were directed to the bureau *ab epistulis* and answering letters were sent directly to the petitioners. Letters were in Latin from the division of the bureau *ab epistulis Latinis* if the petitions had been written in Latin; they were in Greek from the bureau *ab epistulis Graecis* if the petitions had been written in Greek. The recipient might publish the emperor's answer if he so desired. Many of the governors of the provinces made known by edict to the provincial population the contents of the imperial letters (epistulae, *epistolai*).[5] Petitions to the emperor from private persons, on the other hand, were handled by the bureau *a libellis* (bureau of petitions). In that office an answer was drafted and submitted for his approval and signature to the emperor and then appended beneath an officially prepared copy of the petition. The petition with its subscript was next posted at the residence of the em-

---

[2] Otto Karlowa, *Römische Rechtsgeschichte* (Leipzig, 1885), I, 652 n. 1.

[3] Theodor Mommsen, *Juristische Schriften* (Berlin, 1907), II, 178 ff.

[4] Paul Krüger, *Geschichte der Quellen und Litteratur des Römischen Rechts* (2d ed.; Munich-Leipzig, 1912), p. 106 n. 47.

[5] For example, *epistula* of Hadrian, BGU I 140 = *Leges* 78 = *Select Papyri* 213 (119 A.D.); *epistula* of Severus, CIL III 781 = *Leges* 86 (201 A.D.). Further references in Wenger, *Quellen*, p. 428 n. 32.

peror. Professor Wilcken demonstrated that *all* petitions from private persons which the bureau deigned to answer were posted with attached subscript, so that the petitioner or his representative was thus able to read and copy the reply. The evidence showed that a number of petitions with subscripts were fashioned into a roll and the entire roll, or even a number of rolls, were then posted for a time. After some days the roll was removed and filed in the archives, where the petitioner or other authorized parties had access to it at a later date. The official version of the petition with its answer was never transmitted to the petitioner; he could, however, have a transcript made and certified while the rescript was posted or after it had been lodged in the archives.

The views expressed by Professor Wilcken were immediately hailed and accepted by the great majority of scholars.[6] Time and the later discovery of further documents show that the broad lines laid down by that scholar were correct. He himself hesitated to say whether the petitioner had an opportunity to discover the nature of the reply before the petition and subscript were posted. Professor Wenger very recently suggested that the answer might have been given orally in a hearing by the emperor but that the petitioner had to wait for the posting to get the official version and to make a copy if he so desired.[7]

The exceptionally large number of subscripts posted at Alexandria was satisfactorily explained when Dr. Hasebroek showed that the emperor Septimius Severus, with the young Antoninus Caracalla, was in Egypt in 199/200,

---

[6] Meyer, *Zeitschrift für vergleichende Rechtswissenschaft*, 39 (1921), 245 ff.; von Premerstein, "Libellus," *RE*, 13, 34 ff.; Kübler, "Subscriptio," *RE*, 4A, 497 f. Dessau, *Hermes*, 62 (1927), 205 ff., took issue with certain points, to which Wilcken answered, *AP*, 9 (1930), 15 ff. Wilcken's views are now generally accepted; see Fritz Freiherrn von Schwind, *Zur Frage der Publikation im römischen Recht* [Münchener Beiträge zur Papyrusforschung und antiken Rechtsgeschichte, Heft 31] (Munich, 1940), pp. 167 ff.; Fritz Schulz, *History of Roman Legal Science* (Oxford, 1946), pp. 152 f.

[7] Wenger, *Quellen*, pp. 443 n. 192, 445 n. 221. Many years ago, when Professor Ernst Levy had an opportunity to look at P. Col. 123, one of the possibilities he suggested was that the texts represented the stenographic report of the words of the emperor, perhaps later posted in the Fayyum where the petitions originated. Thus the papyrus would be an index of cases reported more fully elsewhere. The writer considered this view but does not believe it accords with the evidence. The Columbia rescripts are actually not more concise than others we have. In view of the fact that it is evident that the subscripts were drafted in Latin and then translated into Greek (see *infra*), the emperor's reply in an oral hearing, if there was one, was made on the basis of the prepared rescript, which subsequently would be posted. At the close of this comment the possibility that all the petitions originated in the Fayyum is considered and discarded.

the year in which most of these rescripts are dated.[8]   The answers or decisions set forth in P. Columbia 123 are said to have been posted in the stoa
of the Gymnasium in Alexandria in March 200.   Two different verbs (*tethen-
tōn* in line 1 and *proetethē* in line 21) are employed to indicate posting.   Both
have the same significance, however, and merely show that the scribe was
supplying his own expression to denote the fact that the texts he was copying were posted.   The question remains as to whether the texts he proceeded
to reproduce were answers of the emperor, subscripts drafted by the bureau
a libellis, in response to petitions directed to the sovereign by private individuals?

COPIES OF APOKRIMATA

The texts which were transcribed from the documents posted in the stoa
were called *apokrimata*.   The verb *apokrinō* from which this form derives
means "to give an answer, to reply to a question."   Forms of this verb are
frequently employed in the papyri to designate the utterances of lawyers,
and sometimes those of the judge, in the reports of trial proceedings which
have added such a living force to our study of the law of Greco-Roman
Egypt.[9]   The nominal form, *apokrisis*, signifies an answer, frequently a decision in a more formal sense.   In contrast, the form *apokrima* is rare.   It
occurs once or twice in Greek literary sources in place of *apokrisis*.   At one
time it seems to have had a more technical meaning, and the problem is
raised as to whether such meaning provides insight into the significance of
apokrimata in our document.

In inscriptions and literary sources of the Greek-speaking provinces of
the Roman Empire it is evident that the answers made in Rome to the
embassies which had been dispatched from the provinces were frequently
termed *apokrimata*.[10]   Thus, for example, there is an answer (*apokrima*)
made by Julius Caesar to a delegation from a city in Greece.   Josephus
relates also that an answer was given by the Roman senate to envoys sent
by Hyrcanus.   Inscriptions of the first and second centuries afford evidence

[8] Johannes Hasebroek, *Untersuchungen zur Geschichte des Kaisers Septimius Severus*
(Heidelberg, 1921), pp. 116 ff.

[9] For example, CPR 18, 15 = Bruns, *Fontes* 189 (124 A.D.); P. Strassb. 22, 13 = *Leges*
85 = *Select Papyri* 261 (200 A.D.).   Cf. Senatus consultum de collegiis artificum 55 = *Leges*
34 (112/11 B.C.).

[10] All the inscriptional and papyrological sources treated in this paragraph are cited and
briefly dealt with, though with a somewhat different interpretation, by Arthur Stein, *Untersuchungen zur Geschichte und Verwaltung Aegyptens unter roemischer Herrschaft* (Stuttgart,
1915), pp. 203 ff.   Cf. also, Egon Weiss, *Griechisches Privatrecht* (Leipzig, 1923), p. 129.

that *apokrima* was used to denote the answer of an emperor to similar embassies. An official was charged with the preparation of such replies. Then in the second century of our era another instance of the relatively rare word occurs in the list of functions of a proconsul, namely, the framing of *epistolai*, *apokrimata*, *diatagmata*. As distinguished from letters and edicts, the "replies" may indeed be answers to petitioners within the province, but whether these were directed to officials or to private persons cannot be determined, of course.

An instance of the word in a semilegal work of the early third century—there is no instance in a strictly legal text—is of particular interest. In a bilingual text prepared for teaching purposes, the so-called *Fragmentum Dositheanum*, the Latin equivalent of *apokrimata* is once given as *responsa*.[11] The text is hopelessly corrupt because the original Latin from which the author made a Greek translation was in medieval times altered to fit the Greek version. Dr. Lachmann attempted a reconstruction of the original text and equated *apokrimata* with *responsa prudentium*, that is, the answers given by Roman jurists to praetor, *iudex* or party litigant. But it has been said that *sententiae* (judgments) is equally valid. Whatever a compiler of bilingual texts for students may have done, the *responsa* of the Roman jurists would never be confused by an imperial chancellery with decisions uttered by an emperor. *Responsiones* is a possibility; *responsa* had a distinct tie with the answers of jurists in the Roman world.

The final instance to be noted of *apokrima* is the one and only occurrence of the word in the published papyri, P. Tebtunis 286. An extract from a judicial record opens with the words: "Extract of the *apokrima* of *divus* Hadrian." The body of the text contains the digests of a series of decisions dealing with unjust possession, though scholars are by no means agreed about the meaning of these decisions within the papyrus. In spite of the uncertainty all but one or possibly two scholars have no hesitation in translating *apokrima* as rescript.[12] Professor Wilcken is again the one scholar

---

[11] CGL III 49, 36: *tōn apo krimatōn* responsorum; in another version, CGL III 102, 23: ex responsis *ex apophthegmatōs*. The reconstruction by Karl Lachmann, *Kleinere Schriften* (Berlin, 1876), II, 203 ff., is queried by Franz Wieacker, *Romanistische Studien* [Freiburger Rechtsgeschichtliche Abhandlungen, V] (Freiburg i. Br., 1935), pp. 67 ff. The Greek and Latin versions of the text are given in Paul Krüger, *Collectio librorum iuris anteiustiniani* (Berlin, 1878), II, 151 f.; the manuscript tradition and Lachmann reconstruction in Ph. E. Huschke, *Iurisprudentiae anteiustinianae reliquias*, 6th ed. Emil Seckel-Bernhard Kuebler (Leipzig, 1918), p. 422.

[12] So by the editors, Bernard P. Grenfell-Arthur S. Hunt, *The Tebtunis Papyri, Part II* (London, 1907), pp. 45 ff.; Mitteis, *SZ*, 28 (1907), 386, and *Chrest.*, intro. to 83; Schubart,

who specifically disagrees with that translation. He points out that *apokrima* in the heading of the Tebtunis papyrus must refer to a judicial decision mentioned in the body of the text. This, like other judicial decisions therein, is termed *apophasis*, the Latin *decretum*. The word *apokrima* was accordingly not the technical term for rescript. We know from scores of papyri that the epistolary form of rescript was *epistolē*, whereas the subscript type was *hypographē*.

The second instance in the papyri is now afforded by the Columbia document, and it supports Professor Wilcken's view. The word *apokrima* means "decision," more particularly, "decision of the emperor," but it is not a technical term for either rescript or *decretum*. It was the intention of the person who used it to designate any type of decision. This person was the scribe in both the Tebtunis case and in the Columbia papyrus. The word was certainly not to be found in the subscripts which were being copied any more than that it was incorporated in the decisions rendered by Hadrian. We feel practically certain of this because scores of rescripts, both epistolary as well as subscript, have been handed down to us in their official forms.[13] An *epistula* always has an epistolary form. A *subscriptio* always opens with the name of the emperor, plus his titles, followed by the name of the addressee (petitioner) in the dative, in short, "Imperator S to X." The answer always follows directly upon this address. Thus, when the scribe of the Columbia papyrus decided to copy a number of subscripts posted on the stoa—he did not choose to copy out the petitions to which the subscripts were appended—he labeled them *apokrimata*, "decisions." He might have called them *hypographai*, "subscripts," for that is what they were, but he may well have wished to emphasize the determinative quality of the answers rather than the form in which they were rendered. The omission of the names and titles of the emperors by the first scribe corroborates this view. Only at a later time did some other person decide to insert the imperial authors in order to indicate the source of these decisions.

Göttingische Gelehrte Anzeigen, 170 (1908), 191; Bortolucci, *BIDR*, 20 (1908), 78; Jörs, *SZ* 36 (1915), 240 n. 2; Wenger, in Johannes Stroux–Leopold Wenger, *Die Augustus-Inschrift auf dem Marktplatz von Kyrene* [Abh. d. Bayer. Akad. d. Wissensch., philos.-philol. u. hist. Kl., 34.2] (Munich, 1928), p. 69 n. 2; Taubenschlag, *SZ*, 70 (1953), 293. Weiss, *SZ*, 33 (1912), 223 n. 4, is cautious, while Wilcken, *Hermes*, 55 (1920), 32 n. 1, says: "*apokrima* später durch *apophasis* ersetzt. Die *apophaseis* . . . können nur Sentenzen, Urteilssprüche in Processen sein." Preisigke, *WB*, s.v. *apokrima*, follows Wilcken, while Arangio-Ruiz, in the republication of the text, *Negotia* 100, translates as *decretum*.

[13] The most significant are republished in *Leges* 72 ff., with an enumeration of other extant rescripts by Adolf Berger, *Leges*, pp. 395 ff.

A fortunate chance enables us to say with no possibility of dispute that these decisions are actually rescripts directed to private individuals (subscriptiones), although not so termed in our papyrus. For the second of our decisions is preserved on another papyrus, P. Amherst 63. It is introduced there in correct subscript form, "Imperator Severus . . . Imperator Antoninus . . . to Artemidorus, also called Achilles." It is interesting to note that the scribe of the Amherst papyrus omitted the imperial names when he transcribed a second subscript, not included within the Columbia group. The scribe of the Columbia papyrus was content to give the names of the addressees, in the dative. This is sufficient to exclude from consideration any type of imperial *constitutio* other than subscript.[14] An edict (*diatagma*) is directed to the whole or to a particular segment of the population; the emperor "says" (dicit, *legei*) is characteristic of an edict, without indication of the group addressed. An *epistula* has the form of a letter; "greetings" (salutem, *chairein*) and "farewell" (vale, *errōso*) are the formal signs of this type of rescript. A judicial decision of the emperor, a *decretum*, is characterized by the pronouncement of the judgment (sententia, *apophasis*); the names of the parties or of the accused are not a vital element. Finally, mandates (mandata, *entolai*) are addressed to provincial governors.

The inescapable conclusion is that all of the "decisions" in P. Columbia 123 are subscripts and thus are addressed to private individuals in accord with the principles established by Professor Wilcken.

THE EMPEROR'S LEGAL ACTIVITY IN ALEXANDRIA

It is not proposed in this comment to discuss the nature of the judicial or other legal activity of Septimius Severus while he was resident in Alexandria in the winter and spring of 199/200. Sufficient material to warrant extended attention to that topic exists both in the papyri listed by Professor Westermann and in related legal, literary, inscriptional, and papyrological sources. It suffices here to offer a few general remarks respecting the persons and the subject matter and then to proceed to comment on the individual rescripts. There are two points tied in with the emperor's presence in Egypt which deserve a few words of comment.

The second line of the prescript of the papyrus contains a date, "year 8, Phamenoth 18" (March 14, 200). Dates regularly given at the close of the

---

[14] Extant constitutions of the emperors collected by Bruns, *Fontes* 77 ff., and in *Leges* 67 ff.

official posted version of a subscript are taken to be the dates when the rescripts were posted. Since the Amherst papyrus which reproduces the second Columbia text is stated to be "Posted in Alexandria, year 8, Phamenoth 18," there is reason to believe that the date in the Columbia papyrus is the date of the posting of the rescripts. It is not the date when the scribe copied the subscripts. The fact that a number of rescripts were posted at the same time lends support to Professor Wilcken's view that a roll of petitions, with appended subscripts, was posted as a unit.[15] The meaning of the interpolated notices in line 21, "likewise posted in the same stoa," and in line 40, "Likewise," are, however, obscure. Are these remarks indicative of the fact that the second and third groups thus introduced were posted at a later date? Or do they mean merely that the scribe returned at later times to transcribe further subscripts? In this connection it is interesting to note that the second of the subscripts in the Amherst papyrus, not included in the Columbia group, is dated six days later, Phamenoth 24.

A question of more general interest is the position of the emperor and of his staff vis-à-vis the normal activities of the prefect of Egypt and of his staff. There is evidence in the papyri that the emperor took over from the prefect as far as judicial functions were concerned.[16] It was the emperor's court which heard cases and rendered judgments. The emperor seems also to have been the author of the subscripts which were posted during his stay. Many of the petitions would normally have been addressed to and answered by the governor of Egypt. It would follow that the staff which prepared the rescripts was an imperial staff rather than the regular staff of the prefect. We know from our papyrus that Plautianus, the praetorian prefect, accompanied Severus to Egypt. There is every reason to believe that at least some members of the bureau *a libellis*, as well as other sections of the secretariat, must also have come to Egypt to handle the affairs of the emperor.

THE RESCRIPTS OF P. COLUMBIA 123 IN GENERAL

Before entering the discussion of the individual rescripts, there are several matters relating to the group as a whole. At this place comment is

---

[15] Wilcken, *AP*, 9 (1930), pp. 19 f.; but cf. Wenger, *Quellen*, pp. 445 ff.

[16] Decisions by the emperor: P. Berol. Inv. No. 7346 vo., ed. H. Frisk, *Aegyptus*, 9 (1928), 281 = SB 7366 (200 A.D.); P. Lond. Inv. No. 2565, 82 ff., 99 ff., ed. T. C. Skeat-E. P. Wegener, *JEA*, 21 (1935), 224 ff. = SB 7696 (c. 250 A.D.); P. Oxy. IV 705, II, 36 ff. Rescripts of the emperor listed by Westermann, *supra*, pp. 26 ff. Cf. generally, Wilcken, *AP*, 7 (1924), 84, and 9 (1930), 22.

devoted to (1) the language of the rescripts, (2) the persons addressed, and (3) the subjects concerned.

In Professor Stein's lengthy discussion of the nature of the Roman administration in Egypt [17] he formulates the principle that rescripts directed to private persons in Egypt (including Romans resident there) were written in the Greek language. Rescripts and mandates directed to Roman officials only were written in Latin. Some scholars accepted this view. Others soon discovered that this rule did not seem always to fit the evidence. Professor Wilcken seems to have doubted the principle from the start and in the course of time took quite a contrary view, eventually coming to the conclusion that *all* subscripts were drafted in Latin.[18] He pointed out that the evidence afforded by *epistulae* had to be excluded, for these were addressed to the petitioner in the language used in the petition. There were bureaus or at least departments *ab epistulis Graecis* as well as *ab epistulis Latinis*. But subscripts were all drafted by a single bureau *a libellis*. Those posted in Rome were in Latin whether the petition was written in Latin or Greek. Seemingly those posted in Alexandria were drafted in Latin but before posting were translated into Greek. It has been demonstrated in a number of cases in recent years that subscripts posted in Egypt and promulgated in the Greek language were actually translations from the Latin. The Columbia rescripts confirm this currently accepted view. Time after time the discussion will reveal that the Greek expressions are direct translations from the Latin and are frequently unknown in the current official or popular usage.

The persons addressed in the rescripts include Greco-Egyptians, Romans, and perhaps others foreign to the province. It has been suggested that petitions might have been addressed to the emperor in Egypt by persons not resident there.[19] We know that when the emperor was in Rome petitioners or their agents journeyed from far afield to present petitions. There is, however, nothing in the Columbia papyrus to show that individuals not regular

[17] Stein, *op. cit. supra*, note 10, 132 ff., 151. In accord: Jouguet, *Revue des études latines*, 3 (1925), 43; John Garrett Winter, *Life and Letters in the Papyri* (Ann Arbor, 1933), p. 33; Oscar William Reinmuth, *The Praefect of Egypt from Augustus to Diocletian* [Klio, Beiheft 34] (Leipzig, 1935), pp. 45 f. Harold Idris Bell, *Jews and Christians in Egypt* (London, 1924), p. 3, found difficulty in applying Stein's principle for he felt that Claudius's letter was a translation from the Latin.

[18] Wilcken, *AP*, 12 (1935), 235; Wilcken, *Atti del IV Congresso internazionale di Papirologia, Firenze 1935* (Milan, 1936), pp. 111 f. In accord: San Nicolo, *Kritische Vierteljahresschrift für Gesetzgebung und Rechtswissenschaft*, 29 (1938), 254 f.; Seidl, *Studia et documenta historiae et iuris*, 4 (1938), 281 f.; Taubenschlag, *SZ*, 69 (1952), 109 n. 33, 118.

[19] Dessau, *Hermes*, 62 (1927), 221 ff.; but cf. Schwind, *op. cit. supra*, note 6, pp. 170 f.

residents of Egypt were among the persons addressed. A woman whose name and patronym may be Semitic and who is represented by her son, also bearing what may be a Semitic name, is the addressee of the fifth rescript. It cannot be said whether they were residents or strangers. If the petitioner was interested in obtaining a copy of the answer, someone would have had to be in Alexandria to obtain a transcription of the posted document or later a copy from the archives.

Most of the rescripts were addressed to single individuals. Those with a plurality of addressees, three in number (Numbers III, VI, and X), were distinctly more administrative than legal in content. It is clear that the questions put affected a larger group and that the petitioners represented others not specifically named. Direct representation of the petitioner is evidenced in three texts (Numbers IV, V, XII). The usual *dia*, "through," indicates the agency.[20] In one case a mother is represented by her son. In another case a father is represented by his son. And in the third case the relation of the agent to the petitioner is not given. In still another case (Number VIII) the petitioner could actually be an agent of the true parties to the question, although there is no direct evidence of such agency.

The subject matter revealed by the rescripts is extremely varied in nature. There are answers which indicate that the questions put to the emperor were concerned with the most complex problems of law. There are others phrased in more general terms which presuppose a much simpler query. Some of the rescripts are in the field of private law. Others deal with subjects today termed criminal. Still others are administrative with the emperor called upon to interpret governmental rulings.

The student of Roman law is accustomed to think of the imperial rescript, at least subsequent to the reform of the bureaucratic structure by Hadrian, as primarily concerned with answers to questions of private law. He takes the rescript as the counterpart of the jurist's *responsum* in the imperial sphere of legal action. The rescripts which are so frequently cited by jurists of the late classical period as well as those which make up the mass of the enactments of the *Codex Iustinianus* both support this position. But it must be remembered that the jurists, as well as the compilers who selected the enactments to be included in the Justinian Code, were interested in the purely legal side of the petitionary procedure, and in the civil rather than

---

[20] Leopold Wenger, *Die Stellvertretung im Recht der Papyri* (Leipzig, 1906), pp. 9 ff., 122 ff.; further references by Taubenschlag, *Law*, p. 386 note *.

the criminal law.   The Columbia papyrus is a refutation of this narrow point of view.   If the emperor at Alexandria was the recipient of administrative and criminal as well as civil law queries, this must also have been true in Rome.

The line to be drawn between the three fields is not a sharp one, at least in the case of Egypt.   Professor Mitteis has warned that frequently one cannot say whether a given procedure is civil litigation, criminal process, or administrative hearing.[21]   In one and the same action there may be both civil and criminal aspects.   So also in the questions put to the emperor. Neither the petitioner nor the chancellery was particularly concerned whether or not the subject matter was what today would be termed civil or criminal or administrative.   The important factor was whether the bureau and ultimately the emperor deemed it worthy of attention.   The Columbia papyrus indicates that the patience of the administration was almost inexhaustible.

The above provides a general background for comment on the individual rescripts.   Each rescript presents problems.   Some of these problems are relatively easy to resolve.   Others must be left temporarily unanswered.   All the rescripts are deserving of further comment.   When all of the rescripts have been canvassed, one point remains for consideration.   Exactly what purpose did this particular scribe have in mind when he transcribed these thirteen distinct subscripts which have come down to us in this papyrus? The attempt to answer this question, in part at least, appears a fitting conclusion to this commentary.

[21] Mitteis, *Grdz.*, p. 24; cf. also Meyer, *Jur. Pap.*, pp. 146, 236 f.

THE SUBSCRIPTS

NUMBER I

5   Ουλπιω Ηρακλανω τω και Καλλινεικω.
      τας επιβληθεισας Αλεξανδρευσι η Αιγυπτιοις ζημι-
      ας δηλωθεν(τα) χρονον προσαγα[γο]ντες ανηκαμεν.

To Ulpius Heraclanus, also called Callinicus.
Having added a specified time, we have remitted
the fines imposed upon Alexandrians or Egyptians.

THE ADDRESSEE (petitioner) of the first rescript of the group in the Columbia papyrus is Ulpius Heraclanus, who is also called Callinicus. That he was a Roman citizen is assured.[22] The combination of a Latin nomen with a Greek or Greco-Egyptian cognomen indicates that he was a Romanized Greek whose original Greek name now appears as his cognomen. The name Ulpius is attested for Roman citizens in Egypt from the first century onward. Consequently, it cannot be determined whether it was Ulpius himself or one of his ancestors who had been granted Roman citizenship. It is known that to obtain Roman citizenship an Egyptian had first to become a citizen of Alexandria. Without further information on Ulpius Heraclanus, his exact civic status must remain somewhat uncertain. The practice of using a by-name, in this case Callinicus, was common in Greco-Roman Egypt, at least among the higher classes.[23] If the petitioner was a Roman citizen, then the question arises: What could have been the nature of the query which led to the reply, "we have remitted the fines imposed upon Alexandrians or Egyptians"?

Some time before the petition, probably in the recent past or perhaps even after his arrival in Egypt, the emperor must have granted a general indulgence of some kind. The indulgence was general insofar at least as it

---

[22] On Roman names and citizenship, see Wilhelm Schubart, *Einführung in die Papyruskunde* (Berlin, 1918), pp. 332 f.; specifically on the name Ulpius, see Taubenschlag, "Rezeption," p. 374 n. 36 [375], and Bernhard Meinersmann, *Die lateinischen Wörter und Namen in den griechischen Papyri* [Papyrus-Institut der Universitätsbibliothek in Heidelberg, I.1] (Leipzig, 1927), p. 90. Alexandrian citizenship as a prerequisite, Woldemar Graf Uxkull-Gyllenbrand, *Der Gnomon des Idios Logos* [BGU V.2] (Berlin, 1934), p. 54.

[23] Calderini, *Aegyptus*, 21 (1941) 221 ff., and 22 (1942), 3 ff., particularly 13 f., 40 ff.

applied to the group known as "Alexandrians" and to that body of the population recognized as "Egyptians." On the acquisition of Egypt by the Ptolemies, citizenship had been granted to the Greek settlers of the city founded at Alexandria and to the Greek inhabitants of the towns of Ptolemais and Naucratis.[24] By the second century of the Christian era, however, the term *Alexandreus*, "Alexandrian," no longer necessarily referred to a citizen but meant also one of the inhabitants whose *origo* was Alexandria. *Origo* denotes the condition of birthright rather than that of residence. Consequently, anyone born of Alexandrian parents had Alexandrian *origo*. The descendants of the original citizens as well as those to whom Alexandrian *origo* was attributed were included within the group known as "Alexandrians." The citizens generally distinguished themselves by employing the appellation of *astoi*, "city-burghers." Foreigners with their own civic status, notably the Romans and the Jews, were resident also in Alexandria but were not "Alexandrians." Then there were also in Alexandria and throughout Egypt the Egyptians and persons of mixed Greek and Egyptian blood who possessed no civic rights whatsoever. These were the "Egyptians" of our rescript. To the Romans they were known as *dediticii*.

Within the permanent population of Egypt there were some other groups ostensibly not included within the terms "Alexandrians" or "Egyptians." For instance, there were the citizens of the autonomous Greek cities of Ptolemais and Naucratis as well as those of Antinoopolis, the city founded by Hadrian. These citizens were on a par with those of Alexandria. Then there was that part of the population known as the Hellenes.[25] The term Hellenes was presumably employed by the Roman government to designate persons possessing the privileges afforded inhabitants of Hellenistic city-states but not affiliated with a particular one in Egypt. Whether the term "Alexandrians" was intended to include the citizens of the Greek cities in Egypt and the Hellenes in general cannot be determined. These people would more likely fall within that group than the class of "Egyptians," if included in either group.[26]

---

[24] On Alexandrian citizenship, Schubart, *AP*, 5 (1913), 104 ff.; on *origo*, Pierre Jouguet, *La Vie municipale dans l'Égypte romaine* (Paris, 1911), pp. 56 ff.; on *astoi*, Taubenschlag, *Law*, p. 11 n. 48. See generally, Taubenschlag, "Citizens and Non-citizens in the Papyri," *Scritti in onore de Contardo Ferrini* (Milan, 1948), III, 166 ff.

[25] Wenger, in Stroux-Wenger, *op. cit. supra*, note 12, pp. 48 ff. The view of Bickermann, *AP*, 8 (1927), 216 ff., that the Hellenes in Egypt possessed no civic status has been challenged by Schönbauer, *SZ*, 49 (1929), 345 ff.

[26] Schubart, *op. cit. supra*, note 22, pp. 260 f. The census returns of the population of a

There is the conspicuous absence of the citizens of Rome from the groups listed in our rescript. The conclusion to be drawn from this fact is obvious. The penalties imposed upon Roman citizens had not been remitted. The purpose of the inquiry by a Roman who was at the same time a citizen of Alexandria can be conjectured. If a fine or penalty of some sort were laid upon him, could he avail himself of the benefit of the imperial pronouncement as an Alexandrian? Or did the fact of his Roman citizenship bar him from such action? The nature of the penalties imposed and now remitted needs discussion before an answer can be suggested.

The word *zēmia* has the general meaning of "penalty" or "punishment," and it has the specific meaning of "fines" in both Greek papyri and Greek literary writings of the Principate. In the papyri, surprisingly enough, the word is scarcely to be found in documents of the second century of our era. In its broader sense *zēmia* corresponds to the Latin *poena*, and as "fines" it is a translation of *multa*. The information we possess from other sources respecting Septimius Severus makes no reference to the imposition of penalties upon Alexandrians or Egyptians for a crime against the state.[27] It is true that Egypt had first sided with Pescennius Niger in the struggle for the throne upon the death of Commodus. But Egypt changed sides shortly after Severus took the field against Niger. We know also that Severus took severe measures against communities which gave aid to Niger. He deprived the citizens of Antioch of many privileges, and he withdrew civic rights from the citizens of Neapolis in Palestine. Many individuals were punished, and communities on Niger's side suffered degradation and fines. Subsequently Severus remitted the penalty imposed upon the Palestinian community. It should be pointed out that the amnesty was a restoration of civic rights and not a remission of fines. Penal fines imposed after the death of Niger would certainly have been collected before the date of this amnesty, which probably occurred during the visit of Severus to Syria in 198/199. The circumstances lead one to conclude that for their political actions the emperor exacted no sums from the Egyptians.

There is more likelihood that Severus granted a general indulgence in the administrative field, namely, a remission of penalties for taxes in arrears,

given locality in Egypt in the second century regularly read: "neither stranger nor Roman nor Alexandrian nor Egyptian . . . is omitted," P. Oxy. III 480 (132 A.D.).

[27] The sources are fully discussed by Fluss, "Severus (13)," *RE*, 2A, 1955 ff., 1959. On the visit of Severus to Egypt, see Hasebroek, *loc. cit. supra*, note 8, and Hannestad, *Classica et Mediaevalia*, 6 (1944), 194 ff.

perhaps even including the sums due. In a papyrus directed to a strategus in 207 A.D. two fugitives who had returned to their lands state, "the emperors Severus and Antoninus, when they were visiting their Egypt, among the numerous favors they granted," also desired that fugitives return to their homes and, accordingly, granted them an amnesty from delinquent taxes.[28] Measures similar in nature were frequent in earlier reigns.[29] Hadrian remitted large amounts of arrears due the fisc, both in the provinces and in Rome. M. Aurelius and later the emperor Aurelian provided the same. In Egypt also, amnesties for fugitives from tax arrears are known; these were pronounced by edict of the governor or of the emperor himself. In none of the above described instances are the tax arrears or the imposed penalties termed *zēmiai* or *multae*. If there is any technical term in the papyri which connotes the penalty for overdue taxes, it is *katakrima*. Nevertheless, such an act of grace on the part of Severus might well be one of the "favors granted," for it certainly would benefit a considerable number of Alexandrians or Egyptians.

Finally, the penalties remitted might have been the fines imposed upon particular individuals in the regular course of criminal trials or administrative proceedings. The visit of the emperor to Egypt might have been the occasion for the exercise of imperial *indulgentia*.[30] It was capital punishment or exile which was relaxed generally, and the property which had been confiscated from the criminal by the state was seldom returned. The remission of ordinary penal fines by an emperor is unknown, to my knowledge. In sum, there are at least two possibilities, tax arrears including penalty and criminal fines. There may be others, but the nature of the *zēmiai* remitted cannot be definitely determined.

The remission granted by Severus was qualified. For the rescript includes the participial clause *dēlōthenta chronon prosagagontes*, literally "having added a specified time," which modifies the words "we have remitted the fines." It appears that the meaning of the clause is that a respite has been

---

[28] P. Catt. II, 6–8 = SB 4284; discussion of this text by Wilcken, *Chrest.*, intro. to 354, and by Lewis, *JEA*, 23 (1937), 66 f.

[29] Imperial remissions: *Script. Hist. Aug.*, Hadrian, 7, 6; Dio 69,8,1 (Hadrian); Dio 72,32,2 (Marcus); *Script. Hist. Aug.*, Aurelian, 39. For Egypt: P. Giss. 40, II, 16 ff. = Wilcken, *Chrest.* 22 = *Select Papyri* 215 (215 A.D.); P. Oxy. XIV 1668, 17–18 (3d cent.); cf. generally, Bell, *Hommages à Joseph Bidez et à Franz Cumont* (Brussels, n.d.), pp. 36 f.

[30] Wilhelm Rein, *Das Criminalrecht der Römer* (Leipzig, 1844), pp. 268 ff.; Contardo Ferrini, *Diritto penale romano* (Milan, 1899), pp. 331 ff.; Theodor Mommsen, *Römisches Strafrecht* (Leipzig, 1899), pp. 484 ff.

granted rather than that there has been a complete release.   There is an interesting parallel for a moratorium of this kind in a rescript of Marcus and Verus which Papirius Iustus digests in his work on imperial constitutions.   The passage reads, "It was also rescripted to the minor that the penalty due the fisc [for taxes due on public lands] would be remitted if he paid the tax within thirty days." [31]   If the situation dealt with in the Columbia rescript is the same as that referred to in the rescript of Marcus and Verus, the "fines" would be the penalties incurred for tax arrears, the second alternative above.   In any case, a definite period of time has been set during which Alexandrians or Egyptians could satisfy their obligations, whatever these might be, and so be absolved from further penalty.   The words *dēlō-thenta chronon* appear to be a translation of something such as *praestitutum tempus*.   There is nothing to indicate the period of time meant.

   This text is left with the questions unanswered.   Indeed, Ulpius himself may not have gained too much satisfaction from the sparse statement made in the subscript.   But then Ulpius and those who cared to read the posted petition knew exactly what question had been asked which we can only conjecture.

NUMBER II

8   Ἀρτεμιδωρ[ω] τω και Ἀχιλλι.
               τοις εγνωσμενοις συνκαταθεμενος βραδεως
               μεμφη τα δοξαντα.

            To Artemidorus, also called Achilles.
               You complain of the decision too late,
            having placed yourself in agreement with
            the findings.

The significance of this second rescript lies in the fact that it is also to be found as the first of the two rescripts published as P. Amherst 63.   The existence of two copies of the same rescript, by two different scribes, affords insight into the particularities of the publication of rescripts and also offers suggestions as to the purpose for which the transcript of these thirteen rescripts was made.   The content of the rescript itself gives little oppor-

---

[31] Dig. 39.4.7.1.

tunity for legal comment. The sense is clear, however: Artemidorus, you have waited too long to complain of the decision for you accepted the findings. It must be remembered that the person to whom the rescript was directed was familiar with the circumstances of the case. The bureau *a libellis* to whom the petition had been submitted also knew these circumstances. Today we possess the brief answer only; hence the meaning of the rescript is enigmatic.

The point that merits attention derives from the juxtaposition of *ta doxanta* and *tois egnōsmenois*. The meaning of these two participial nouns is relatively similar—"decisions" of some type or other. The former, *ta doxanta*, was used in Attic Greek to signify what was the "pleasure" of a public body, that is, "resolution." The papyri of the Roman period present this form only rarely, but it is attested for the "resolution" of a municipal senate in third-century documents.[32] In a second-century record of a trial it can mean nothing other than the "decision" of the prefect.[33] In the context of our rescript *ta doxanta* appears to have the meaning of a final judgment from which Artemidorus has no appeal.

The petitioner has no further recourse because he has delayed too long and by nonaction at least, has implicitly accepted the findings which had been made earlier. The term *egnōsmena* is literally "what has become known," and it occasionally means "judgment" or "decision" in literary writings. But in the papyri, at least in Ptolemaic times, it reveals its basic meaning. Administrative texts of the middle of the second century B.C. speak of "results" of land inspections, *ta egnōsmena ex episkepseōs*.[34] These are apparently the same kind of land inspections referred to in the sixth rescript of our papyrus. It is not suggested that the imperial chancellery used a term in the sense it had been used some three hundred and fifty years earlier, for it does not appear to have persisted in this connotation. Rather, the form used was a direct translation of the Latin *cognita*. This latter word was current in the familiar expression *causa cognita*, the hearings in a magisterial investigation. The investigative proceedings played an extremely important role in Roman Egypt. Administrative and police actions form the bulk of the hearings in which the magistrate undertakes an examination of the circumstances of the case (*causa cognita*), but the noncontentious civil pro-

---

[32] P. Oxy. XII 1414, 4 (270–275 A.D.) and possibly P. Oxy. XIX 2228, 31 (283 A.D.).

[33] P. Gradenwitz, ed. K. Galm = SB 5693, 21 (186 A.D.).

[34] P. Teb. I 82, 2 = Wilcken, *Chrest.* 232 (115 B.C.), and P. Teb. I 149 (116/115) B.C.). Cf. P. Teb. I 72, 193, 201 (114/113 B.C.).

ceeding and even party litigation had their share of "findings." One cannot say what interlocutory "findings" Artemidorus had failed to take exception to, but the period had elapsed within which he might have appealed to higher authority. He is therefore bound to abide by the final "decision."

NUMBER III

11   Αυρηλιοις Αρτεμιδωρω και Ανουβιωνι και αλλοις.
        τοις εγνωσμενοις πιθεσθαι.

       To the Aurelii Artemidorus and Anubion and others.
        Obey the findings made.

The shortest of the rescripts refers to *egnōsmena* which, in the light of what has just been said, presumably means administrative "findings." The petitioners are told to obey, nothing more and nothing less. In this case however, it is to be noted that at least two, if not all, of the petitioners are Roman citizens. The name Aurelius is a frequent nomen of Romanized Greeks even before the *constitutio Antoniniana*.[35] There is no reason to believe, of course, that a Roman citizen should be treated differently from anyone else in an administrative hearing.

NUMBER IV

13   Κιλ.[..]δις τω και Μιδα δια Φιλοκρατους υιου.
       ωσπερ ανατραπηναι την πρασιν των υποθη-
       κων ου δικαιως αξιοις ουτως απολαβειν σε [[σου]]
       την νομην των χωρις συνβασεως κατεχομενων
                                      σι.

       προς βιαν χωριων ο ηγουμενος του εθνους κελευ

       To Cil...dis, also called Midas, through Philocrates, his son.
         Inasmuch as without right you request that
       the sale of the hypothecated properties be rescinded,
       the prefect of the province will order that you re-
       cover possession of the plots held by force without
       agreement.

[35] Taubenschlag, "Rezeption," p. 374 n. 32, and *supra*, note 22.

This rescript, which deals with the procedure to be followed as a result of the sale of mortgaged properties (*prasis tōn hypothēkōn*), is one of the most interesting and at the same time one of the most difficult rescripts to interpret. The first difficulty stems from the fact that one cannot be certain what particular type of real security was involved in the original transaction. Greco-Roman Egypt, unlike Rome, knew a wide variety of devices enabling persons to make loans on the security of real property. Yet it is necessary to select the particular form which lay behind the procedure described in the rescript. Each form of real security had its own particularities. Each form offered certain courses of conduct for creditor and debtor to follow upon repayment of the loan or upon default. The problem is to eliminate the types failing to fit our rescript. Then, having selected the most probable one, it will be possible to present the situations which would form the basis of the question put and the answer made.

Professor Ludwig Mitteis's brilliant portrayal of Greco-Egyptian "Pfandrecht" some forty years ago, confessedly incomplete and in part hypothetical, is still the best presentation of this subject.[36] Supplementary studies considering newly published sources have substantiated his views and added variations only within the recognized types. This approach to "pledge-law" serves as the basis of the following discussion.

Perhaps the oldest type of real security in Greco-Roman Egypt, which seems to derive from the Egyptian law, was a sale conditioned upon the payment of a loan. During the first century B.C. and the first century of the Christian era this transaction was accomplished by the simultaneous execution of two documents, a contract of loan and a deed of sale.[37] Reference is made to a contract "of sale and of mortgage and of loan" in a document of the middle of the second century.[38] This may be related to that type of transaction. But the simultaneously executed documents are not found after the first century of our era, while the reference in the second-century docu-

---

[36] Mitteis, *Grdz.*, pp. 129–165. The results of earlier studies are incorporated in Mitteis's presentation. Important publications of later date by Schwarz, Raape, and others are listed in the bibliographies to the articles by Manigk, *RE*, s.vv. *hypallagma*, *hyperocha* and *pignus*, but the views expressed by Manigk in these articles are not in accord with those generally accepted. Ziebarth, "Pfandrecht (Hellenistische)," *RE*, Supp. 7, 981 ff., is too brief to be of much value. A recent summary by Taubenschlag, *Law*, pp. 205 ff., with supplement in *AHDO/RIDA*, 1 (1952), 321 ff.

[37] References in Taubenschlag, *Law*, pp. 205 n. 3, and 206 n. 4.

[38] P. Lond. II 358, p. 172 = Meyer, *Jur. Pap.* 83. The fictional hypothecated loan is a device to enable the vendor to gain the purchase price by summary proceedings, so Mitteis, *Grdz.*, pp. 117 n. 2, 122 f.; Jörs, *SZ*, 39 (1918), 97 f., 117 f.; Meyer, *loc. cit.*

ment is to sale plus fictional hypothecated loan. The "sale *of* hypothecs" in our rescript cannot be the "sale *and* mortgage-loan" of this early type of real security.

The reference in the rescript is also not to the transaction known as *ōnē en pistei*.[39] This is a fiduciary transfer of ownership. Title passed with the loan, and there was a right, indeed a duty, of recovery upon repayment. But the element of trust (fiducia, *pistis*) is all-important in this transaction, and it presumably would be mentioned if this was our transaction. In addition, the *ōnē en pistei* was relatively infrequent in the second century. Further, there is no connection between the "sale of hypothecs" of the rescript and the institutions of *enechyron* (pledge) of movable property or the various forms of *antichrēsis*, which gave the creditor the use of the property, save insofar as the *antichrēsis* was supplemental to the forms about to be described.

There remain, then, the two most important types of real security, *hypothēkē* and *hypallagma*. In the strict forms of these contracts there is a sharp distinction between the two institutions. The transaction is a *hypothēkē* where it was expressly stipulated that the property "fell" to the creditor upon failure to repay a loan. Possession of the property usually remained with the debtor, and evidence of title passed to the creditor. Upon default the creditor was able to obtain possession by a relatively simple taking with official sanction (*embadeia*). When the creditor was given a conditional right of execution upon the property of the debtor at the time the loan was made, however, the transaction is a *hypallagma*. The debtor remained in possession but specifically renounced his right of alienation. Upon default the creditor gained title by state-supervised execution upon the property (*enechyrasia*), followed by officially supervised entry into possession. As an alternative the creditor might proceed against the person of the debtor by levying execution upon the whole of his property. A hybrid type of transaction combined elements of both *hypothēkē* and *hypallagma* and gave the creditor an election of remedies.[40] The petitioner in our rescript is not a Roman so the peculiarities of *hypothēkē* or *hypallagma* when executed by a Roman citizen need not be considered.

Between these two, *hypothēkē* and *hypallagma*, the choice must fall on the first. *Hypallagma* was indeed a lien on the land and there might be reference

[39] References in Taubenschlag, *Law*, p. 206 n. 7. Many scholars consider the *ōnē en pistei* to be related to the simultaneously executed documents noted above, see intro. to P. Ryl. II 160(c) (32 A.D.). Cf. also, Wenger, *Quellen*, p. 759 n. 265.

[40] Schwarz, *Aegyptus*, 17 (1937), 241 ff.

to hypothecation in documents relating to the *hypallagma* transaction.[41] But if the imperial chancellery speaks of the "sale of hypothecated lands" the likelihood is that lands encumbered by *hypothēkē* were involved. The transaction which lay behind the plea of the petitioner has been determined. We may now turn to the rescript itself. In sequence the following points are presented: (1) the action attempted was without right, incorrect, for (2) the petitioner had sought to rescind the sale of hypothecated lands; instead, (3) by order of the prefect the petitioner could recover the possession of the properties (4) held by force and without agreement. It is proposed to comment upon these points in succession, thus eliminating the improbable situations in the course of the discussion and eventually arriving at a recognition of the status of the petitioner and the meaning of the rescript. The various possibilities which are explored and discarded may offer to others a point of departure for a different solution.

"Inasmuch as without right you request" are the opening words, in the English translation at least. The term *axioō*, "to request," is the prevalent technical term employed by a petitioner seeking the aid of a magistrate, "I petition, I request." It is the counterpart of the Latin *postulare*, to seek an action or remedy before the Roman praetor or magistrate. And when the magistrate, upon the statement of the circumstances made by the petitioner, decides that the relief desired is not available, the answer may well be *contra ius postulas*, "you request without right," or some similar expression.[42] The emperor in our rescript answers in exactly the same way, namely, that the petitioner is seeking the wrong remedy for the recovery of his property.

The action sought had been a rescission of the sale of the mortgaged plots. *Anatrepō* indicates the revocation of a unilateral transaction such as a donation, or the rescission of a bilateral agreement such as a sale.[43] Just why it was improper to seek to rescind the sale depends for its answer on the determination of who were the parties to the sale, when it took place, and, specifically, who was the petitioner who sought the rescission. In summary

[41] For example, P. Lond. II 311, 13, p. 219 (149 A.D.); cf. Andreas B. Schwarz, *Hypothek und Hypallagma* (Leipzig-Berlin, 1911), pp. 56 ff. Land charged with *hypothēkē*, e.g., P. Bas. Inv. 7, 19, ed. E. Rabel = Mitteis, *Chrest.* 245 = SB 4434 (time of Hadrian); P. Oxy. III 653 desc. = Mitteis, *Chrest.* 90,13 (160–162 A.D.).

[42] In the Codex Iustinianus, for example: Cod. 3.1.7 and 6.20.13: *contra ius (iura) postulas*; Cod. 3.38.4, 4.2.15 and 9.22.19: *contra formam iuris postulas*; Cod. 2.18.11: *non iuste ratione postulas*.

[43] In the Basilica *rescindo* is regularly translated by *anatrepō*, e.g., Bas. 24.7.6 = Cod. 4.16.6; Bas. 25.7.7 = Dig. 20.5.7.1.

outline the possible situations can be presented and the choice narrowed. The sale of the mortgaged lands took place either (1) while in the possession of the debtor before the due date of the loan, (2) while in the possession of the creditor during that time, or (3) while in the possession of the creditor after foreclosure. The person seeking rescission of the sale, the petitioner, could have been either the debtor (*D*) or the creditor (*C*); it is unlikely that the purchaser of the property (*P*) was the petitioner.

1 (a). *D* is in possession, *C* has title. If *D* sells the land to *P*, he is violating the explicit or implicit restraint on alienation. *P* might indeed purchase but could not register the transfer of property. When *C* discovered a sale had been made of lands belonging to him, he might seek to rescind. Thus *C* as a petitioner is *possible*.

1 (b). *D* cannot be the petitioner seeking to rescind a sale by *C* to *P* because *C* had no possession to transfer.

2 (a). *C* is in possession and has eventual right to clear title. *D* cannot sell to *P*, having neither possession nor evidence of title.

2 (b). *C* can fraudently sell to *P* land which he does not yet fully own. *D* is not in a position to complain until he tenders the sum due or actually repays the loan. But when he offers to repay the loan, he is entitled to recover the property and thus might seek rescission to regain the land. Petition by *D* is *possible*.

3 (a). Upon default, *C* has by relatively simple procedure gained possession. *D* has thus neither title nor possession to transfer to *P* by a sale. *C* could not thus be the petitioner.

3 (b). *C* has both title and possession and consequently could sell without hindrance to *P*. But in so doing he would violate the fundamental nature of the *hypothēkē*, a substitute-pledge: the land for the money. There may well have been what can be termed an equity of redemption, so claim for rescission by *D* may have been made and petition by *D* is *possible*.

For the moment, then, Cil...dis, the petitioner in our rescript, is either (1) the creditor before the loan is due, (2) the debtor on tender of payment, or (3) the debtor after foreclosure. To the petitioner the emperor answers that rescission of the sale is not the proper remedy. The reason seems to be the same with respect to all three: the petitioner is not a party to the contract of sale. The Greco-Egyptian law of sale recognized a few special situations in which the parties could rescind a sale.[44] It is not even certain that a

[44] Fritz Pringsheim, *The Greek Law of Sale* (Weimar, 1950), pp. 497 ff.

minor or a judgment-creditor could annul a contract fraudulently made by the guardian or by the judgment-debtor. The fact that there could be no rescission did not mean, however, that a person was denied relief who had been deprived of his property by the fraudulent act of another. The late classical Roman law, particularly as evidenced in the rescripts of the emperors to the eastern provinces, provides for the recovery of property so lost.[45] In our rescript relief is also provided.

"The prefect of the province will order that you recover possession of the plots." The order of the governor of Egypt would be directed to a subordinate magistrate, the latter to act in judicial, investigative, or administrative capacity.[46] One cannot say whether trial, investigation, or administrative action is proposed. It is true that the petitioner has presented one side of the case only in his petition, and the present occupant may have a sound legal basis for his possession. For that reason normal judicial action may have been meant. On the other hand, the command of the prefect may signify direct action by the designated magistrate. The rescript merely says *apolabein tēn nomēn*, "recover possession," which indicates any type of *in rem* proceeding.

Against whom is the proceeding to be directed? The rescript says, against the person who "held by force without agreement." The phrase *pros bian* represents the Latin *vi*, "by force." The possessor has no legal justification for his possession, yet retains forcibly against the demands of the complainant. For this reason we may eliminate from consideration one of the three cases enumerated above, namely, the attempted action by the creditor before the loan is due. For the possessor in that case was the purchaser of the lands, and even though he may have acquired possession without title he cannot be said to be holding "by force." For this reason also, we may say that in each of the two possible remaining suits, namely, by the debtor either before or after foreclosure, the contemplated action was against the creditor and not against the purchaser. In the one case, sale before the due date of the loan, the purchaser bought property which the creditor was occupying and for which he could show certificates of title. In the second case, sale after foreclosure, the purchaser bought property which the creditor was occupying and for which he had clear title. Perhaps it was even recorded

[45] Wilhelm Felgentraeger, *Antikes Lösungsrecht* [Romanistische Beiträge zur Rechtsgeschichte, Heft 6] (Berlin-Leipzig, 1933), pp. 13 ff., summary, pp. 25 ff.

[46] Reinmuth, *op. cit. supra*, note 17, pp. 89 ff., has summarized the types of delegated authority.

in the registry. In neither case, if the purchaser were now in possession, could he be said to be holding it against the claims of the petitioner "by force."

It follows, therefore, that the creditor-mortgagee is in present possession.[47] If he refuses to turn over the property to the debtor either upon tender of the money due or upon exercise of a power to redeem after foreclosure, the creditor who will not surrender is holding "by force."

There are two published papyri which present situations in accord with those just described, and, though neither is exactly the same as those offered by our rescript, they indicate that either of these situations is a possibility. The first papyrus is a petition to a strategus dated in the time of Vespasian.[48] It is addressed by three sons who declare that their father had borrowed a sum of money from a certain Leonides and had mortgaged land by *hypothēkē* to secure the loan. The mortgagee received the crops, and according to the sons the loan had been repaid. Leonides nevertheless sold the property to a bona fide purchaser, claiming that there was a further debt due him from the father. The sons informed the purchaser that the sale was invalid, but the creditor had already requested the authorities to execute upon the property for satisfaction of the debt. The sons now ask for a suspension of the execution proceeding until a suit can be instituted. The situation is of interest in that the sons are apparently about to sue the creditor for disposing of property which was not yet fully in his ownership.

The second papyrus reveals a situation paralleling that raised by our rescript if the sale occurred after foreclosure. The document is the report of a hearing before the prefect in 160–162.[49] As security for a loan the debtor mortgaged his property by *hypothēkē* to the creditor. Upon default the creditor was permitted, after court judgment in an action for payment, to execute upon the property and gain possession. A sale of the mortgaged properties was ordered upon the intercession of other persons, claiming to be further

---

[47] According to Pringsheim, *op. cit. supra*, note 44, pp. 219 ff., transfer of possession is not required for transfer of ownership. It is not even mentioned in contracts of sale, cf. Mitteis, *Grdz.*, p. 188. Hence, the purchaser of the mortgaged property may have left it in the possession of the creditor.

[48] P. Berol. 11808 + P. Oxy. IX 1203, ed. Sigurd Möller, *Griechische Papyri aus dem Berliner Museum* (Diss. Göteborg, 1929), p. 28 = SB 7339. Cf. Wilcken, *AP*, 9 (1930), 247; Felgentraeger, *op. cit. supra*, note 45, pp. 74 f.

[49] P. Oxy. 653 desc. = Mitteis, *Chrest.* 90; cf. Felgentraeger, *op. cit. supra*, note 45, pp. 70 f., and Jörs, *SZ*, 39 (1918), 54 ff. Other instances of equity of redemption, P. Catt. vo. = Mitteis, *Chrest.* 88 (c. 140 A.D.), cf. Jörs, *SZ*, 39 (1918), 99 ff.; P. Ryl. II 119 (54–67 A.D.), cf. Jörs, *SZ*, 39 (1918), 55 n. 3.

creditors of the debtor. At that point the debtor intervened, and with a tender of the money owed demanded the return of the property. The remainder of the proceeding deals with a dispute as to the interest on the loan. But important for us is the fact that the prefect ordered the creditor to return the property. Failure to do so would not only result in judgment against him but he would be flogged in addition.

The petitioner in our rescript is the debtor. The person against whom the remedy is available is the creditor. No choice can be made as to whether the debtor is provided with a remedy before the debt is due or is granted relief by way of equity of redemption after foreclosure. The mention of the fact that the property is held *chōris synbaseōs*, which is the Latin *sine conventione*, "without agreement," is of no help in making a decision. It could mean without an agreement between creditor and debtor, giving the former a right to dispose of the property before payment was due. Or it could mean that the parties had by agreement waived the debtor's equity of redemption. We must be satisfied with the fact that the choice of possible situations raised by the rescript has been narrowed down to two.

NUMBER V

18

...θαλγη Αμβρηλου δια Αβδομανχου υιου.
αργυριον γυναικες δανιζεσθαι και υπερ αλλων
εκτινιν ου κωλυονται.

To . . .thalge, daughter of Ambrelus, through
Abdomanchus, her son.
Women are not forbidden to borrow money
and to pay in behalf of others.

In a simple straightforward way the emperor replies to a woman who has petitioned through the agency of her son. There is no prohibition against women borrowing money and paying for others. There must have been some idea in the mind of the petitioner about to engage in a business transaction involving the transfer of money that there was some limitation on the capacity of women to act in this fashion. The basis for this idea is the subject of this comment. What the emperor said and what he implied by omission is part and parcel of the discussion.

It is well established that in the Greco-Egyptian law of Roman Egypt there was no limitation on the capacity of women to take part in any sort of private or commercial transaction.[50] Indeed, one of the remarkable characteristics of the Greco-Egyptian law was that in the field of private law women stood on an equal footing with men. It is true that frequently women acted through the agency of a man, a husband or a son or a guardian. But this was no limitation on their ultimate power to enter into whatever type of transaction they wished. As a matter of fact the guardian was largely a straw figure. The woman in business was quite free, and there is not the slightest evidence of actual curtailment of her capacity by reason of the presence of a guardian. She entered into marriage of her own will, and neither custom nor law prevented divorce. She could act as guardian of her own children or of others, and *materna potestas* was as significant as *paterna potestas*. The papyri illustrate all types of transactions by women, including loans and mortgages in connection with loans.

Why then, should any woman in Egypt raise a question as to her capacity to act? The answer may be that the particular woman who asked the question was aware of the fact that some women resident in Egypt did not have capacity to engage in all private legal transactions. These were women citizens of Rome.

Roman law, even by the second century of our era, was by no means on a par with Greco-Egyptian law so far as the rights of women were concerned. In the private law, although there had been a partial emancipation in the late Republic, there were significant disabilities of Roman women which continued throughout the Principate.[51] There were limitation on their rights in succession. They could not act as guardians of minors. But the language of our rescript has clear reference to a particular disability: that created by the *senatus consultum Velleianum* of the early years of the Principate.[52]

[50] Schubart, "Die Frau im griechisch-römischen Ägypten," *Internationale Monatsschrift für Wissenschaft, Kunst und Technik*, 10 (1915/16), 1503–1538. Neither L. Bringman, *Die Frau im prolemäisch-kaiserlichen Aegypten* (Diss. Bonn, 1939), nor Iza Biezunska, *Études sur la condition juridique et sociale de la femme grecque en Égypte gréco-romaine* [Hermaion, fasc. 4] (Lvow, 1939), save for a review of the latter by Ciapessoni, *Athenaeum*, 18 (1940), 206 f., was available.

[51] Paul Gide, *Étude sur la condition privée de la femme* (2d ed.; Paris, 1885), pp. 123 ff. Briefly, Fritz Schulz, *Principles of Roman Law* (Oxford, 1936), pp. 208 f. For gains in the late Republic, see Wilhelm Kroll, *Die Kultur der Ciceronischen Zeit* (Leipzig, 1933), II, 26 ff.; Fritz Schulz, *Classical Roman Law* (Oxford, 1951), pp. 182 ff.

[52] Literature cited by Berger, *ED*, s.v. *Senatus consultum Velleianum*. Recent works, cited therein, have reopened the question as to the extent to which loans in behalf of others were prohibited; the words of the *senatus consultum* are simply: *pro aliis reae fieri*.

A reactionary body, such as the Roman senate was shortly after the end of the Republic, reaffirmed in this *senatus consultum* the old principle that a woman was not capable of undertaking *officium virile*, the duties to be undertaken by a man. It proceeded on this basis to invalidate legal transactions in which women obligated themselves in behalf of others. Construing this enactment the Roman jurists proceeded to develop the concept of *intercessio mulieris*, which broadly meant that no legal act was valid which entailed liability for a debt not of economic benefit to the woman. Thus, a woman could not act as surety for the debt of another nor obligate herself by a loan where the purpose was merely to transfer the sum of that loan to another person. If the purpose of the transaction was solely to pursue her own affairs, however, the *senatus consultum* was not involved. The jurist Ulpian says, "Hence, when [a woman] wishes to make a gift to Titus [the third person], if she has borrowed money from me and given it to Titus, the *senatus consultum* does not apply." [53] Donations by women, whatever the manner in which they were brought about, were not invalidated by the enactment. Gaius, in his comment on the provincial edict, says, "It makes no difference whether [the woman] paid out money for the purpose of discharging a debt or has given any of her property in satisfaction thereof; even if she had sold her property and paid the price received for it in behalf of another, . . . I hold that the *senatus consultum* will not apply." [54]

The answer of the imperial bureau is completely in line with the jurists' interpretation of the *senatus consultum Velleianum*. It is perfectly proper for a woman to borrow money. There is nothing to show that the obligation incurred is not to her own interest. It is permissible to pay money in behalf of others. This is a beneficence on the part of the woman, not an obligation. The conclusion is inescapable. The rescript is framed in the light of Roman law. This type of transaction is not forbidden. It is clearly implied that other transactions are forbidden, to wit, those which fall within the scope of the *senatus consultum*. The petitioner contemplated borrowing money to pay another's debt.[55] The bureau had a ready answer provided by the Roman law: this is not forbidden.

[53] Dig. 16.1.4.1.

[54] Dig. 16.1.5. Cf. also, Cod. 4.29.1 (212 A.D.).

[55] This combines the two clauses of the rescript into one transaction; it is, of course, possible that separate transactions were contemplated. A subscript may afford answers to more than one legal question, provided these are raised by the circumstances in the petition, e.g., Cod. 7.8.1 and 8.25.1, a single rescript to Proclus (205 A.D.). Cf. Theodor Kipp, *Geschichte*

But why would the answer of the emperor be phrased in the scope of Roman law? In this case the answer would have been the same if Greco-Egyptian law had been applied, namely, there is no prohibition. The first explanation coming to mind is that the petitioner was a Roman citizen. But this will not fit. Professor Westermann has indicated that the names of the petitioner and her son may point to a Semitic origin. There is nothing to indicate that she is a Roman citizen; indeed, the contrary is more likely. On the other hand, neither is it likely that she was Greco-Egyptian, either a citizen of Alexandria or Greek city-state in Egypt or an Egyptian noncitizen. For it has been pointed out that neither city-state nor folk law knew any limitation upon the powers of women to transact their own affairs. A woman of any one of these groups would not be apt to put the question to the emperor.

A citizen of a foreign state or a foreign noncitizen resident in Egypt might well be uncertain what her position was. The imperial bureau, temporarily in Egypt, would hardly attempt to discover the rights afforded a woman in a particular foreign legal system. From its point of view, the Roman law provided a satisfactory answer to the petition. That was the legal system known to the staff. Its rules could be applied and afford justice to all subjects of the Empire. These hypotheses raise the broader question whether the doctrine of *intercessio mulieris* was in the process of being transformed from an institution of the Roman *ius civile* into an institution applicable to all throughout the Empire, or at least throughout the province of Egypt. It is unnecessary to pursue this idea further in view of the fact that, to the writer's knowledge, there is no evidence that the *senatus consultum Velleianum* or the law developed by the interpretation of the jurists was applied to any but Roman citizens during the epoch of the Principate.

In sum, this rescript indicates that, to a petition inquiring as to the capacity of a woman to engage in a particular legal transaction, the emperor—in actuality the bureau *a libellis*—answered in the scope of the classical Roman law.

---

der Quellen des römischen Rechts (4th ed.; Leipzig, 1919), p. 74: "Reskripte . . . in welchen der Kaiser sich über die auf die Sache anwendbaren *Rechtssätze* ausspricht [italics mine]."

NUMBER VI

22   Α]πολλωνι Αρνεκτωτου και αλλ[ο]ις.
      αι περι των επισκεψεων. κρισις κοινη παρεσχεν
      προνοιαν Αιγυπτιοις.

To Apollo, son of Harnektotes, and others.

The queries (?) concerning inspections. A common decision has given consideration to Egyptians.

The subject matter of the answer posted for the benefit of Apollo and other persons cannot be determined with any degree of certainty. The word *episkepsis* means "inspection," but exactly what type of inspection is difficult to determine. As Professor Westermann has pointed out, the reference is quite probably to the inspections made in connection with land surveys since this is the most frequent type of *episkepsis* mentioned in the papyri of any epoch. The possibility exists that "inspections" or indeed "investigations" of another type are meant. Further uncertainty results from the omission of the noun introduced by the feminine plural article *hai*. It would seem that some such word as *aiteseis*, "requests," is to be understood. From the legal point of view nothing more need be said of the opening phrase.

The utilization of the words *krisis* and *koinē*, both of which have a broad variety of connotations, offers field for comment. The word *krisis* serves to designate a decision of any kind, by magistrate, by judge, or, indeed, by private persons. Fortunately, the scope may be narrowed to decision by the emperor or decision by the prefect of Egypt. The chancellery would make no reference to decision by a lower official and it may be that even the person of the prefect should not be included. The direct reference to Egyptians, however, merits the inclusion of the latter official.

Decisions of emperor or of governor were made in judicial hearings (decreta) or in rescripts addressed to officials (epistulae) or to private persons (subscriptiones). It is true that any pronouncement of emperor or governor might loosely be termed a decision. One would then be inclined to add decision by edict even though the technical term *diatagma* was not employed. For, as is apparent, the technical terms for *decreta* or rescripts were also not used. Edicts and *decreta* and rescripts did not have to be labeled. Each had its own particular form and was so recognized. The basic idea behind *krisis* is that it derives from *krinō*, "to judge," and can be correctly employed to indicate a *decretum* or a rescript or even the two together in the sense of pronouncement. But the idea of "judging" is not in any way indicative of the nature of an edict, which is "speaking forth, ordering." There is only one instance in the papyri where *krisis* is used to designate an imperial order. In one case the word is used to signify the orders of Decius to participate in religious rites among more than twenty-five documents of the same type in which the normal words for "orders" or "edicts" have been employed.[56] The usage is at least abnormal if it is not incorrect. *Krisis* regularly stands for "decision" by emperor or by governor in the papyri.

The decision is described as a *krisis koinē*, "common decision," in our rescript. No similar combination of *krisis* and *koinē* has been found. But the meaning is clear: the decision is common because it is applicable to all Egyptians. This brings to mind the comparable concept of an imperial enactment of general application known to the Roman law, *constitutio generalis*. The earlier view of scholars was that enactments of emperor and governor had no validity beyond the reign or term of office of the sovereign or of the official promulgating them.[57] It was further declared that *decreta* and rescripts were valid for the instant case alone and had merely persuasive force in the decision of future cases. Now it has been demonstrated that edicts of emperors and governors were valid under succeeding rulers and officials and were binding legal orders until specifically abrogated.[58] It has further been argued and generally accepted that the decisions of emperor and governor are binding precedents, not merely persuasive in nature.[59] *Decreta* and re-

---

[56] P. Oxy. XII 1464 (250 A.D.). All the Decian *libelli* are republished by Knipfing, *Harvard Theological Review*, 16 (1923), 345 ff. References to the so-called *libelli libellatici* by Wenger, *Quellen*, p. 420 n. 160, and specifically in the Decian prosecution, Wenger, *BIDR*, 45/46 [postbellum] (1951), 45 n. 2.

[57] Theodor Mommsen, *Römisches Staatsrecht* (3d ed.; Leipzig, 1887), II, 911 ff., 1124; Moriz Wlassak, *Kritische Studien zur Theorie der Rechtsquellen im Zeitalter der klassischen Juristen* (Graz, 1884), pp. 150 ff.; Krüger, *op. cit. supra*, note 4, pp. 113 f. Cf. also, Kipp, *op. cit. supra*, note 55, p. 68 n. 14.

[58] Orestano, *BIDR*, 44 (1936–1937), 219 ff., on the edicts of emperors; Wilcken, *SZ*, 42 (1921), 124 ff., on the edicts of provincial governors.

[59] Riccardo Orestano, *Il potere normativo degli imperatori e le constituzioni imperiali* (Rome, 1937), pp. 61 ff.; De Robertis, *Annali della Facoltà di Giurisprudenza*, n.s., 4 (1942), 3 ff., 281 ff. Accord: Max Kaser, *Römische Rechtsgeschichte* (Göttingen, 1950), pp. 133 f.; cf. also Schwind, *op. cit. supra*, note 6, pp. 148 ff., and Fritz Schwind, *Römisches Recht I* (Vienna, 1950), pp. 61 f. On the validity of imperial enactments in Egypt as portrayed by the papyri, see Taubenschlag, *SZ*, 70 (1953), 293 ff. On the validity of prefectural decisions, see Wenger, *Actes du Ve congrès international de Papyrologie, Oxford 1937* (Brussels, 1938), pp. 551 ff.

scripts of the emperor and the decisions of the governor which were intended to have general application were valid both in time and space—subject, of course, to the territorial jurisdiction of the official rendering them. It was not until the end of the second century that the Roman jurists fully accepted this doctrine, and it may be that the references to *decreta* and rescripts as *generales* are postclassical interpolations. But whether or not they were termed "general," the jurists would have no difficulty in determining which decisions were intended to have general force and which were to be limited to the particular case to which they were directed. A recent article by Professor Steinwenter has given the proper perspective to this entire subject.[60] Imperial decisions of general nature were valid and binding precedent for all future cases of similar content. The same was true for decisions of a governor within the territorial extent of the province. The significant factor is that a rule laid down in a general decision need not be applied unless the new case was "on all fours" with the previous decision. The doctrine *could* be extended by analogy to the new case if the judge so desired. If the case concerned the same legal circumstances, the rule of the former decision *had* to be applied.

The papyrological and inscriptional evidence fully supports this position. In the first place it is quite simple to distinguish those rescripts to private persons intended to apply only to the case to which they were directed. The Columbia papyrus itself contains instances of special as well as of general rescripts. A rescript of Septimius Severus on *longae possessionis praescriptio* was intended to have general application.[61] On the other hand, a rescript of a prefect of Egypt assigning the complaint of a petitioner who alleged unlawful liturgical services to a subordinate official for investigation is an instance of a decision limited to the particular case.[62] The same is true of rescripts to officials and of *decreta*. The decision of the emperor in the litigation between the Falerians and the Firmani is clearly for that case only, while the decision of Severus on exemption from liturgies was held to be binding some fifty years later.[63] The prefectural decisions so often cited by attorneys in later cases established binding rules, while other decisions filed in the

[60] Artur Steinwenter, "Prologomena zu einer Geschichte der Analogie II: Das Recht der kaiserlichen Konstitutionen," *Studi in onore di Vincenzo Arangio-Ruiz* (Naples, 1952), II, 169 ff., particularly 175 ff., 182 f.

[61] BGU I 267 and P. Strassb. 22 = *Leges* 84-85 = *Select Papyri* 214 and 261 (200 A.D.).

[62] P. Oxy. XVII 2131, 19 ff. = *Select Papyri* 290 (207 A.D.).

[63] Falerian-Firmani case: CIL IX 5420 = *Leges* 75. Decision of Severus: P. Lond. Inv. 2565, 82 ff., 99 ff., *cit. supra*, note 16; cf. Wenger, *op. cit. supra*, note 59, pp. 537 ff.

records of the governors were decisions for particular cases.[64] Determining whether the general decision served as binding precedent and furnished the rule of law for the future case rested upon the extent of agreement between the new case and the old. In the litigation on liturgical exemptions in which the above-mentioned decision of Severus was urged as precedent, an attorney argued that the *decretum* need not be applied because conditions had radically changed since the imperial decision was made. The prefect decided, however, that the emperor's decision was binding upon him and provided the rule for the case then in litigation.

The rescript in the Columbia papyrus informs the petitioners that an earlier decision—whether imperial or prefectural, *decretum* or rescript cannot be said—had laid down a rule of general application for all Egyptians. The ruling on particular matters regarding inspections made in that earlier case was a binding precedent for their cases and for all others of similar nature in which Egyptians were involved.

NUMBER VII

25   Ἀυρηλιω Σαρ[α]πιωνι.
    τας γενο[μ]ενας εκ μητρωου γενους εις δια<κα>τοχην
    κατερχεσ[θ]αι πρωην εκωλυσαμεν.

To Aurelius Sarapion.
    Some time ago we forbade that the patrimony (?) coming
from the maternal side [of the family] come down in succession.

The seventh rescript in the Columbia papyrus is in answer to the petition of a Roman citizen, Aurelius Sarapion. The name Aurelius was the normal indication of the grant of Roman citizenship by the *constitutio Antoniniana* in 212 A.D. Even before that time, however, the name Aurelius serves to indicate a Romanized Greek. This status has been earlier described in the case of Ulpius Heraclanus, in the comment to the first rescript of the papyrus.

The answer by the emperor to the petitioner may, for the purposes of this discussion, be divided into three topics: (1) what was the petitioner seeking, (2) in what fashion was it being sought, and (3) what was the earlier action of the emperor.

---

[64] As binding precedents, see Jolowicz, *Journal of the Society of Public Teachers of Law* (1937), pp. 7 ff., and Steinwenter, *loc. cit. supra*, note 60. Decision for the instant case alone: P. Oxy. I 40 = *Select Papyri* 245 (2d cent.).

The opening Greek words are to be translated "those (?) coming from the maternal stock (side of the family)." The crucial noun introduced by the article *hai* has been omitted, exactly as it occurred in the previous rescript. This was probably not due to an oversight on the part of the scribe. It was not inserted by the chancellery for there could be no question as to what was meant. Some word for patrimony or property, such as *ousiai*, is to be supplied. It is also possible that *klēronomia*, "inheritance," was understood,[65] though actually the property sought was not technically an inheritance in that it had not been left to the petitioner by will. The property which the petitioner seeks to obtain by intestate succession is obviously that which belonged to his mother's blood relations, normally, to his maternal grandparents. In the Latin draft such property would be termed *bona materni generis*.

According to the Roman system of intestate succession which was based on the Twelve Tables, children could never be called as successors to their mothers. They did not fall within any of the three recognized classes, namely, those who had been in the power of the deceased (sui), those descended from the same male ancestor (adgnati), or those members of the same organized unit (gentiles). It was not until well along in the second century of our era that a radical change was made in this system of intestate succession. By a *senatus consultum Orfitianum* of 178 A.D.[66] children were counted in the first class (sui), in taking upon the death of their mother dying intestate. The child could thus succeed to the mother's property (bona materna) but not to that of his maternal stock (bona materni generis).

Alongside the civil law intestate succession, the Roman praetor had built up a separate system of intestate succession, *bonorum possessio*. Those children entitled to succeed according to the *senatus consultum Orfitianum* were also entitled to seek the estate by *bonorum possessio*, subsequent to the date of that enactment. But they were only granted praetorian succession in the second class of claimants, subsequent to the group which would have been entitled under the civil law succession if they had not been released from the paternal power of the deceased, for example, emancipated children.

The position of children with respect to the succession to their mother's

---

[65] Hans Kreller, *Erbrechtliche Untersuchungen auf Grund der Graeco-Aegyptischen Papyrusurkunden* (Leipzig-Berlin, 1919), p. 124 n. 3, notes the incorrect usage of *klēronomia*, but cf. Arangio-Ruiz, *Negotia*, p. 186 n. 1.

[66] For the reason of the enactment, see William Warwick Buckland, *A Text-Book of Roman Law from Augustus to Justinian* (2d ed.; Cambridge, 1950), pp. 373 f.

estate in Greco-Egyptian law was quite different from that described for the Roman law.[67]   In Greek as well as Egyptian law children had been entitled to share in the estates of both parents, from Ptolemaic times on.   By the second century of the Christian era this had been expanded to cover the right to succeed to the property of grandparents.   A grant by the emperor Hadrian affirmed this principle with respect to the maternal grandmother's estate for the Greco-Egyptian inhabitants, and prefectural decisions extended the rule to include the Egyptian population.[68]   In another papyrus of the same epoch the *bona materni generis* is the subject of litigation.[69]

It can be seen that our petitioner might be uncertain whether he, a Roman citizen of Greek origin, was entitled to share in the proceeds of his maternal grandparent's estate.   The emperor turned him down.   As a matter of fact, it was almost two centuries before an imperial enactment granted to Roman citizens the right to succeed to the estates of their maternal grandparents.[70] It is of interest to the student of Roman law to note that the expression *bona materni generis* is not to be found in the Digest and appears only in the rubric of a title of the Theodosian and Justinian Codes.[71]   The imperial enactments set forth in these titles, the earliest of which date from the reign of Constantine, do not use the expression, and consequently it is not repeated in the corresponding title of the Basilica.   Yet at the beginning of the third century, as our rescript shows, the Greek equivalent of the Latin was used by the imperial chancellery.

The emperor answers that *bona materni generis* shall not "come down into succession," *eis diakatochēn katerchesthai*.   It has long been recognized that the word *diakatochē* was used to reproduce in Greek the Latin *bonorum possessio*.[72]   An application for *bonorum possessio* was directed to the governor, who acted in the place of the praetor in affording this type of intestate

---

[67] See generally, Kreller, *op. cit. supra*, note 65, pp. 141 ff.; briefly, Taubenschlag, *Law*, pp. 138 ff.

[68] BGU I 19 = Mitteis, *Chrest.* 85 (135 A.D.).   The interpretation of this papyrus is a matter of dispute, reference in Mitteis, *Chrest.* 85, and Taubenschlag, *JJP*, 6 (1952), 123.

[69] P. Rein. 44 = Mitteis, *Chrest.* 82 (time of Hadrian).   Discussion of this and the case in the previous note, Kreller, *op. cit. supra*, note 65, pp. 160, 162 f.; Taubenschlag, *JJP*, 5 (1951), 127 f.

[70] Cod. Theod. 5.1.4 = Cod. 6.55.9 (389 A.D.); cf. Inst. Iust. 3.4.1.

[71] Cod. Theod. 8.18 and Cod. 6.60.   An equivalent, *avi materni bona*, is found in the Theodosian and Justinian codes, but the exact phrase *bona materni generis* occurs only in the rubrics and perhaps in a reconstructed text, Cod. Theod. 8.18.4 (339 A.D.), yet it is a familiar technical expression among the Pandectists, e.g., Bernhard Windscheid, *Lehrbuch des Pandektenrechts*, 9th ed. Theodor Kipp (Frankfurt, 1906), III, 69 f.; cf. Vincenzo Arangio-Ruiz, *Istituzioni di diritto romano* (11th ed.; Naples, 1952), pp. 477 f.

[72] De Ruggiero, *BIDR*, 14 (1902), 101 ff.; cf. further, Preisigke, *Fachwörter*, s.v. *diakatochos*, and Kreller, *op. cit. supra*, note 65, pp. 58 ff.   Instances of the term among *agnitiones bonorum*

succession to Roman citizens in Egypt. The application had to be in Latin, but it might contain a Greek docket or other notation; the whole might be translated into Greek for use in registering property so received. And the term *diakatochē* regularly replaces (*bonorum*) *possessio* in these situations.

Is the petition, then, a request for information as to the petitioner's rights by way of *bonorum possessio*? If so, he would be entitled to take only after persons in the first class—provided there were any—had failed to apply within the required time. As already noted, the *senatus consultum Orfitianum* placed children in the first class of persons (sui) entitled to succeed to *bona materna* under the civil law of intestate succession. The petitioner would certainly prefer to be included within the *sui*, rather than take by praetorian succession, if the emperor was disposed to extend the right of succession to *bona materni generis*. If that is so, *diakatochē* means *possessio* in the sense of a civil succession rather than a praetorian *bonorum possessio*. This accords with the view that, in a papyrus referring to a declaration of intestate succession of children to the mother's estate made for the purpose of estate taxation, the words *hereditatem seu bonorum possessionem* is mere notarial caution, for civil intestate succession in accord with the *senatus consultum Orfitianum* is clearly envisaged.[73]

The emperor answered that the petitioner was not entitled to take the property of his maternal grandparents. "Some time ago we forbade" are the words of the rescript. The action in the rescript, accordingly, is not a first decision but followed an earlier determination, presumably made by Severus himself. The form in which the idea of prohibition is expressed, by the word *kōluō*, "to forbid," three times in this one papyrus, is perhaps indicative of a more general type of imperial enactment, in other words, by an edict rather than by a *decretum* or a rescript. Words of command are characteristic of the edictal form; the negation of command is probably the same.[74] It seems that nothing more precise may be said than that the emperor had declared himself unwilling to extend the benefits of the *senatus consultum Orfitianum* to include *bona materni generis*.

---

possessionis: P. Giess. Inv. No. 40, ed. Eger, *SZ*, 32 (1911), 378 ff. = Meyer, *Jur. Pap.* 27 = *Negotia* 61 (249 A.D.), fully translated into Greek, P. Iand. 253, ed. Kalbfleisch, *SZ*, 64 (1944), 416 ff.; P. Oxy. IX 1201 (258 A.D.), cf. Wenger, *Quellen*, p. 826 n. 1042. In declarations for inheritance tax purposes or registration: P. Amh. II 72 = *Negotia* 62 (249 A.D.); P. Oxy. XIX 2231 (241 A.D.). Cf. generally, Wenger, *Quellen*, pp. 825 f.

[73] P. Oxy. VIII 1114 = *Negotia* 63 = *Select Papyri* 326 (237 A.D.). Cf. comment of Kreller, *op. cit. supra*, note 65, p. 124 n. 3.

[74] Wilcken, *SZ*, 42 (1921), 141 n. 2.

NUMBER VIII

28 Π[ρ]οκλω Απολλ[ω]νιου.
    τους γεγρ[α]μμενους κληρονομους (και αι διαθηκαι
    τε̣ιλασθαι λεγωνται) της ν[ο]μης ουκ εστιν
    δικα[ι]ον εκβληθηναι. φρον̣τ[ι]σουσιν δε οι
    τα̣[s] δικ̣α̣ς επιγεγραμμενοι καλεσαι τους
    ευ̣[θ]υνομενους ει γε το πραγμα εστιν εν τη
    ταξει των διαγνωσεων.

To Proclus, son of Apollonius.

It is not right—if the testament is said to be per-
fect—that heirs written [in the will] have been deprived
of possession. Those [charged with] inscribing cases
shall take care to cite the accused persons if the matter is in the order of inquisitory trials.

The rescript devoted to the relief of heirs deprived of their inheritance is
provocative but, like so many rescripts in the papyrus, it cannot be con-
clusively interpreted. The circumstances leading to the inquiry are perfectly
clear. On the other hand, the procedure suggested by the emperor gives rise
to a number of possible explanations. The comment describes the situation
and focuses attention upon the hypothetical solution which appears to best
accord with the language.

The petitioner is a certain Proclus. The name Proclus is one sometimes
borne by Roman citizens, but the omission of a cognomen makes it unlikely
that such is the case here. Nor can it be said that Proclus is a freedman on
the basis of his Latin name. It is apparent, though, that he is probably not
one of the persons directly involved in the alleged wrongful action.[75] He is
acting as agent or as a friend in petitioning the emperor.

The designation of the injured parties as *gegrammenoi klēronomoi* is a
literal translation of the Latin *heredes scripti*, "heirs named in a will." This
can only mean that these persons were designated as *heredes* in a Roman
will. And as such they were entitled to enter into the inheritance if they so
desired. But they have been unlawfully deprived of their due. The word
ekballō literally means "to throw out," but it is not believed that physical

---

[75] Proclus may, of course, have been appointed *heres suus* or *heres necessarius*, see Berger,
ED, s.vv., but it is not believed so.

dispossession is necessarily involved. It could mean that there had been deprivation of rightful possession of an inheritance by any illegal act of a third person. The exact nature of the expulsion is, in the writer's view, indicated by the remedy suggested in the rescript.

Before proceeding to that question a few remarks may be offered regarding the parenthetical clause in the first portion of the rescript. Although the reading is apparently clear, the scribe has written *kai* instead of *kan*, "and if." [76] The use of the plural *diathēkai* does not mean that more than one will or even copies of a single will are referred to, but rather that reference is made to the external form of the will, *tabulae testamenti*, "tablets of the will." The tablets of the will are said to be *telasthai*, "completed, perfected." This is the Greek rendition of the Latin *perfectum*. A will in which all the rules of form have been observed is a *testamentum iure perfectum*, "a will legally valid." [77] The sense of the situation is that if the will is alleged to be formally valid the heirs designated therein cannot legally be deprived of possession of the inheritance.

The remainder of the rescript is devoted to a statement of the procedure to be followed by the heirs to remedy the wrong they have suffered. Just what this procedure entails is so succinctly delineated that it is difficult to state with any certainty the form of process which is involved. It is possible to offer a plausible solution with an analysis of the three factors which are introduced in the answer of the emperor. The three factors stressed in the latter portion of the rescript are: (1) persons are charged with registering cases, (2) the accused shall be cited, and (3) the matter shall be in the "order" of inquisitory trials.

The middle voice of the verb *epigraphō*, in participial form, can be rendered in English as "those inscribing," that is, the officials charged with registering the complaints. The notion of inscribing cases brings to mind a characteristic element of the Roman criminal procedure. Criminal process in the late Republic was instituted by a complaint to the proper authority. [78]

[76] Required by the mood of the verb.

[77] For example Dig. 29.3.2.1 and 48.10.6 pr.; Cod. 3.28.16. Further instances, Hellmann, *SZ*, 24 (1903), 66 ff.

[78] The procedure here described is that outlined by Moriz Wlassak, *Anklage und Streitbefestigung im Kriminalrecht der Römer* [Sitzb. d. Akad. d. Wissensch. in Wien, philos.-hist. Kl., 184.1] (Vienna, 1917), pp. 6 ff. The nature of the preliminary process is disputed, see Gustav Geib, *Geschichte des römischen Criminalprocesses bis zum Tode Justinian's* (Leipzig, 1842), pp. 281 ff.; Mommsen, *op. cit. supra*, note 30, pp. 381 ff.; Naber, *Mnemosyne*, n.s., 28 (1900), 440 ff., but it is unnecessary to enter into that point here. Specifically, on *libellus inscriptionis*, Carl Georg Bruns, *Kleinere Schriften* (Weimar, 1882), II, 52 ff.; Pfaff, "Inscriptio in crimen," *RE*, 9, 1561; Premerstein, "Libellus," *RE*, 13, 59 ff.

On preliminary hearing the accuser named the person he accused (delatio nominis) and briefly outlined the charges. This was done by presenting a formal signed petition (libellus inscriptionis) requesting the inscription of the name of the accused in the registry of criminal cases. If the official believed there was reason to warrant criminal action, he accepted the complaint and duly inscribed the name of the accused (nomen recipere) in the register of cases set for trial. At the proper time the trial took place before a jury. This was the accusatory procedure of the late Republic.

Early in the Principate a new criminal process came to the fore. This was the so-called "inquisitory" process, a proceeding under the control of a state magistrate from start to finish. Many of the actions within this process continued to be introduced by private accusation. The practice of petitioning the magistrate to inscribe the name of the accused was thus employed whether the procedure was accusatory or inquisitory in nature. The writings of the jurists of the time of the Severi reveal that the details of the private accusation remained much the same as they had in the last century of the Republic.[79]

In the provinces the inquisitory procedure had been used from the beginning. There also private accusation introduced certain criminal actions. The magistrate was the governor, to whom criminal competence had been delegated by the emperor. He frequently assigned the investigation of criminal affairs to subordinate officials and might even turn the entire trial over to another. It is therefore suggested that minor officials were charged by the prefect of Egypt with the registration of the names of alleged criminals upon the petition of private accusers. In our rescript the injured parties were advised to initiate a criminal process in a manner which had long been established both in Rome and throughout the provinces of the Roman Empire.

The magistrate or the official who listed the name of the accused and thus established the sequence of trials was also charged with summoning him to court for the adjudication of the charges brought. In the papyri the term kaleō means "to summon," whether the summons is directed to a defendant in a civil or administrative action or to an accused in a criminal trial. Coupled as the word is with tous euthynomenous, "the accused persons," in our rescript, the reference is clearly to citation in a criminal suit. If further evi-

---

[79] Paul, Dig. 48.2.3 pr., gives the form of the *libellus inscriptionis* at the beginning of the third century. Cf. also, Ulpian, Dig. 48.5.2.8 and 45.5.18.1; Cod. 9.1.2 (205 A.D.). See generally, Wlassak, *op. cit. supra*, note 78, pp. 87 n. 14, 89 ff.

dence were needed to show that the inscription (registry) of cases was indeed
the preparation of the criminal calendar, it is afforded by this portion of the
reply of the emperor.

The final clause of the rescript notes that the remedy proposed, namely,
private accusation and trial of the persons who have deprived the heirs of
possession of the inheritance, would be available only if the matter were, to
use a Latin rendition of the Greek, *in ordine cognitionum*. If the previous
points are well taken, the term *diagnōsis* (cognitio) refers to the whole of the
criminal action.[80] There was no *cognitio* in the true accusatory procedure
because the investigation and decision of the case rested with a jury. In the
inquisitory procedure, however, a magistrate supervised the introductory proceedings, conducted the trial, determined the guilt or innocence of the accused, and uttered the sentence. *Diagnōsis* thus means the criminal case in
the inquisitory proceeding.

When attention is turned to the other component of the phrase, *taxis*
(ordo), two suggestions may be made.[81] The word may mean "good order,
regular procedure," and in the instance of our rescript thus signify the proper
observation of the inquisitory process. Such a remark on the part of the
emperor would, however, seem superfluous. In a more primary sense *taxis*
means "sequence," and in legal writings it is frequently used in this connotation. This meaning is favored here, particularly as the phrase recurs in
comparable context in an imperial edict dealing with appeals in criminal
proceedings. A Latin papyrus, the date of which is uncertain, contains the
words (reconstructed in part): [*lites ex or*]*dine cognitionu*[*m*] *offici nostri*,
"cases from the sequence of inquisitory trials of our bureau." [82] The sequence of the criminal calendar is to be observed in handling appeals. In our
rescript, adopting this meaning, the recording magistrates would summon the
accused in accordance with the listing in the registry of accused persons.

The three factors presented in the latter portion of the rescript have been
described. A type of criminal process introduced by private accusation conducted as a normal inquisitory proceeding by a magistrate is suggested by

[80] Kleinfeller, "Cognitio (2)," *RE*, 4, 218 ff.; Lauria, *Atti della R. Accademia di Scienze
morali e politiche di Napoli*, 56 (1934), 308 ff. Berger, *ED*, s.v. *Cognitio*: "In criminal matters
cognitio covers the whole proceeding, judgment included."

[81] As inquisitory process, note the rubric Cod. 7.19: *de ordine cognitionum*, and see Sachers,
"Ordo," *RE*, Supp. 7, 796 f. Otto Ernst Hartmann-August Ubbelohde, *Der Ordo Iudiciorum
und die Judicia extraordinaria der Römer I* (Göttingen, 1886), pp. 543 ff., summarizes the
various meanings of *ordo* in the legal field, with "sequence" the first to be discussed.

[82] BGU II 628 ro. 14 = Mitteis, *Chrest.* 371 = *Leges* 91; further references in *Leges*, p. 452.

the emperor. Is it possible to specify the particular criminal action which the emperor had in mind? Since a Roman will forms the basis of our petition, Roman legal remedies would presumably be suggested in the answer of the emperor. Most of the remedies available to an heir in the Roman law are excluded from consideration by reason of the criminal nature of the procedure which has been outlined. Neither the interdicts nor the *hereditatis petitio* come into question. Nor, since the substance of the crime is given, have we to do with any of the offenses against the state, against the person, or even against property save testamentary. In fact, the circumstances fit but one remedy, the *crimen* (or *accusatio*) *expilatae hereditatis*, "crime of plundering an inheritance." [83]

Until well into the Principate there was nothing to prevent another person from taking possession of property not yet occupied by the heir. There could be no theft of testamentary property, and there was no reason why the possessor could not acquire title after possession for the prescribed length of time. A *senatus consultum* enacted during the reign of Marcus Aurelius changed this situation. An heir, either before or after acceptance of the inheritance, was permitted to institute criminal proceedings against a person who had taken possession of the property of the inheritance. Since this was a criminal action, presumably any person could institute such a suit, but normally the accuser would have been the potential or actual heir. The *crimen expilatae hereditatis* was classed among the so-called *crimina extraordinaria*, that is, a crime which was established subsequent to the period when the so-called "statutory" crimes had been formulated. As such the magistrate conducting the trial was free to fix the nature and extent of punishment as he thought suitable for the particular case. Although information is lacking, we may be sure that if there was a conviction the heir gained possession of the property which had been occupied by the criminal.

A papyrus dated in 295 A.D. is a petition to the prefect of Egypt relating in detail the theft of property belonging to the estate of the petitioner's mother.[84] As intestate successor the complainant requested that an action be granted against the criminals, clearly a *crimen expilatae hereditatis*. The rescript of P. Columbia 123 illustrates a stage in an identical procedure, almost a century earlier in time. With a copy of the rescript from the em-

---

[83] Dig. 47.19 and Cod. 9.32; reff. to secondary literature, Berger, *ED*, s.v. *Crimen expilatae hereditatis*. Add Mommsen, *op. cit. supra*, note 30, pp. 777 ff., and Giuseppino Ferruccio Falchi, *Diritto penale romano (I singoli reati)*, (Padua, 1932), pp. 230 ff.

[84] P. Oxy. VIII 1121 = *Negotia* 186.

peror as authorization, the heirs may request the inscription of the names of the possessors of the property as accused persons and then formally petition for the criminal action.

In addition to the fact that the substance and process of *crimen expilatae hereditatis* accord with all the information given in the rescript, there are passages which are pertinent in the writings of the jurists of late classical times. Ulpian, in his treatise on the office of the provincial governor, says, "If a *crimen expilatae hereditatis* is brought, a provincial governor ought to grant his own inquisitory process (suam cognitionem); since an action of theft is not available, the assistance of the governor is all that remains." [85] The jurist is as solicitous of the cause of the "plundered" heir as was the emperor in our rescript. It is further interesting to note that the jurist Marcian cites a rescript of Severus and Caracalla offering the heir an election between *crimen expilatae hereditatis* and the civil action "to recover an inheritance from the possessors by the ordinary law." [86] Does this mean that Severus concluded that the remedy he offered in our rescript was inadequate and that he subsequently granted the heir a choice of civil or criminal action? There is no answer to this, of course. But as far as our rescript is concerned, the advice Proclus was given to pass on to the heirs was that they should institute a *crimen expilatae hereditatis* if and when the recording magistrates were willing to set the case down for trial.

NUMBER IX

35 Κρονιω Ηρακλειδου.
  αι προσκαιροι νοσοι των πολιτικων ουκ απαλλασου-
  σιν λιτουργιων και οι ασθενεις δε τω σωματι λιτουργ-
  ουσιν εαν τη φροντιδι των οικιων πραγματων
  εξαρκιν δυνωνται.

To Cronius, son of Heraclides.
 Temporary sicknesses do not excuse from civic liturgies, and those physically sick are subject to liturgical services if they are able to undertake the care of their own affairs.

[85] Dig. 47.19.2 pr.
[86] Dig. 47.19.3.

The rescript directed to the petitioner who sought exemption from liturgical services requires no lengthy comment as far as its substance is concerned. Petitions for excuse from obligatory tasks are well represented in the papyri of second-century Egypt. Of interest in this comment is the fact that the expressions and phraseology of the rescript are reflected in the sources of the Roman law. The Greek work which is most extensively extracted in the Digest is the treatise on "Excuses from Guardianship" by Herennius Modestinus, and therein are to be found frequent references to *politikai leitourgiai*.[87] Elsewhere in the Digest there are passages enumerating the various types of burdens imposed on individuals at the end of the second century.[88] The papyri and the legal sources together indicate that the rules respecting liturgical services were largely of general application throughout the Roman Empire.

The Columbia rescript lays down a criterion for excuse from liturgical service on the plea of sickness. There is no excuse "if those physically ill are able to undertake (suffice for) the care of their own affairs." This measure of fitness also appears to be a rule of the imperial law. In the course of the treatise written by Modestinus for the benefit of the officials and lawyers of the eastern provinces, an extract from the jurist Ulpian is quoted, "Sickness also excuses but it is a hindrance only if one cannot carry on his own affairs."[89] The Latin clause *quo minus quis suis rebus superesse possit* is an exact counterpart of the Greek in the rescript. Ulpian goes on to say, "as our emperor with his father rescripted." It would have been a striking coincidence if the rescript on papyrus were the one quoted by Ulpian, but Ulpian then deals with further matters contained in his rescript. Nevertheless, it is clear that the bureau *a libellis* had established a rule of thumb to measure the extent of illness which would serve as a valid excuse. Such a rule was not limited in its application to the province of Egypt but was applied elsewhere throughout the Empire. It was certainly applied in those provinces in which a relatively similar system of liturgical duties was in force.

[87] For example, Dig. 27.1.2.6, 5.12, 6.3, 8.3.

[88] Dig. 50.4.1.2 contains a lengthy enumeration. For exemption, see Dig. 27.1 *passim*; Dig. 50.4.3 ff., and in the papyri, sources discussed by Hohlwein, *Museé Belge*, 12 (1908), 89 ff.; Wilcken, *Grdz.*, 344; Friedrich Oertel, *Die Liturgie. Studien zur ptolemäischen und kaiserlichen Verwaltung Aegyptens* (Leipzig, 1917), pp. 390 ff.

[89] Dig. 27.1.10.8 i.f.

NUMBER X

41   Διοσκ[[ο]]ωρω Ηφαιστιωνος και Πιεσηϊ Οσιριος
      και αλλοις.
      αργυριον αντι πυρου καταβαλλιν υμας εκω-
      λυσαμεν.

> To Dioscorus, son of Hephaestion, and to Pieseis, son of
> Osiris, and others.
> We have forbidden you to pay money in place of grain.

In the view of the writer there is little necessity at this point for further
comment on this rescript. The suggestion made by Professor Westermann
that a number of petitioners have sought permission to pay their taxes in
money in lieu of grain seems the most plausible one to offer. As indicated
in the historical comment, the prohibition of *adaeratio* has a significant meaning in the reign of Septimius Severus. There is a possibility, of course, that
the rescript was in answer to a request for a legal ruling on the substitution
of money payment for grain in the performance of private obligations. But
the wording of the rescript militates against this view. Since no information
is available for discovering the actual circumstances that led to the petition,
little more can be suggested.

NUMBER XI

45   Ισιδωρω Δειου.
      τα μεν απο Κομωνος τετολμημενα
      Φλουειος Πλαυδιανος ο κρατιστος επαρχος
      των στρατοπεδων και οικειος ημων
      εξετασι. προς δε Απιωνα τον τελωνην ει μη
      κοινωνι των ενκλημ[α]των Κομωνι, τον
      ηγουμενον του [ε]θνους ε[ξ]εις δικα[σ]την.

> To Isidorus, son of Dius.
> Fulvius Plautianus, His Excellency the Prae-
> torian Prefect and our household companion,
> will investigate the audacious actions [emanat-
> ing] from Comon. With respect to Apion, the
> tax-farmer, if he is not involved in the charges
> against Comon, you will have the prefect of
> the province as judge.

One of the most interesting of the thirteen decisions of the emperor is that appointing Fulvius Plautianus, the praetorian prefect, to investigate charges made against a certain Comon and designating the prefect of Egypt to hear the case against a tax-farmer named Apion. The rescript further directs that, if Apion is implicated with Comon, Plautianus shall have the investigation of both. Isidorus, the petitioner, has undoubtedly suffered grievous injury at the hands of Comon, and Apion may have had a part therein. Isidorus seeks redress for the injury. There is no way of determining whether Isidorus was mulcted of money or deprived of property, but the harm must have been outrageous in character since the emperor named the highest officials of the Empire to handle the matter.

The identification of Apion as *telōnēs*, "tax-farmer," indicates that the wrong resulted from malpractices in the collection of taxes farmed out by the state. Before the Christian era both Egypt and Rome extensively resorted to the practice of auctioning off the right of collecting specified taxes to the highest bidders.[90] A partnership of capitalists (*telōnai* with *metochoi*, *societas publicanorum*) was the usual successful bidder. With the advent of the Principate a change in government policy took place. The farming-out of state taxes remained a method of raising the revenues of the Roman state, but direct collection by the state occupied more and more of the field. Securing bidders was difficult, and from the time of Trajan a limited number of indirect taxes only were farmed out, including customs duties, tolls, and passport fees.[91]

As a result, the papyri of second-century Egypt offer little evidence of the institution. Among the rare references are documents dealing with malpractices in the actual collection of the taxes on the part of tax-farmers or their associates. A petition to the strategus complains that *telōnai* had at-

---

[90] The basic study on tax-farming in Ptolemaic Egypt is to be found in Ulrich Wilcken, *Griechische Ostraka aus Aegypten und Nubien* (Leipzig-Berlin, 1899), I, 515 ff. On tax-farming in Republican Rome, see Ferdinand Kniep, *Societates publicanorum* (Jena, 1896).

[91] The edict of Tiberius Iulius Alexander, prefect of Egypt, of 68 A.D., declared that force would not be resorted to in order to carry through tax-farm auctions, CIG III 4957, newly edited by Oliver, in H. G. Evelyn White–James H. Oliver, *The Temple of Hibis in El-Kārhgeh Oasis, Part II: Greek Inscriptions* [Publications of the Metropolitan Museum of Art, Egyptian Expedition, Vol. XIV] (New York, 1938), No. 4, 9–15. Nevertheless, bids were still difficult to obtain, P. Oxy. I 44 = *Select Papyri* 420 (end 1st cent.); note also another plea against compulsory farming out, in a rescript of Hadrian, Dig. 49.14.3.6. Generally on tax-farming in Egypt during the Principate: Wilcken, *op. cit. supra*, note 90, pp. 570 ff.; Michael Rostowzew, *Geschichte der Staatspacht in der römischen Kaiserzeit bis Diokletian* [Philologus, Ergänzungsband 9] (Leipzig, 1902); Sherman LeRoy Wallace, *Taxation in Egypt from Augustus to Diocletian* (Princeton, 1938), pp. 286 ff.

tempted to exact payment of a tax even though a receipt for payment was shown them.[92] And more significant, perhaps, is the edict of a prefect of the middle of the second century directed against the practice of exacting money from transient visitors not subject to the tax.[93] The Columbia papyrus reveals that extralegal acts of tax-farmers had not abated. Although there is no direct reference to Comon as a partner or associate of Apion in a group which had acquired the collection of the taxes, a connection between the two is apparent. Plautianus is to investigate Comon, the governor to hear the case against Apion, and the former is to handle both provided there was complicity on the part of Apion. The "audacities" or "effronteries" (ta tetolmēmena) of which Comon is accused coincide remarkably with Ulpian's remarks about tax-farming partners in general: "There is no one who is not aware of how much audacity and how much malice are the contracts of the tax-farmers; hence the praetor promulgated this edict for the purpose of checking their audacity." [94]

The audacious acts of Comon were to be investigated by Plautianus, the praetorian prefect. Possibly Comon was an individual high in the hierarchy of Egyptian officials. He may have ranked equal with the prefect of Egypt, though that is unlikely for he was a non-Roman, as the name indicates, and non-Romans were rarely if ever included among the highest state dignitaries. Whatever the position of Comon, if the emperor attributed judicial competence to the praetorian prefect, it presents a heretofore unknown situation in the annals of the Roman Empire. In recent years several scholars have traced the rise in power of the prefect of the praetorian guard to a position second only to that of the emperor.[95] By the era of Severus the praetorian prefect was highest in military command. He accompanied the emperor on his campaigns and, if the latter desired, might even hold the position of commander-in-chief. He was the key official in the administration of military justice, and the military administrative organization was under his control. There is the possibility that the provisioning of the city Rome was also placed under his supervision by Severus. By the end of the second century

---

[92] BGU I 340 (148 A.D.).

[93] P. Princeton A.M. 8931, ed. O. W. Reinmuth, *Classical Philology*, 31 (1936), 146 ff. = SB 8072; republished as P. Princ. II 20 (middle 2d cent.).

[94] Dig. 39.4.12.

[95] Marcel Durry, *Les Cohortes prétoriennes* [Bibliotheque des Écoles françaises d'Athènes et de Rome, fasc. 146] (Paris, 1938), pp. 147 ff.; Alfredo Passerini, *Le coorti pretorie* [R. Istituto Italiano per la storia antica, fasc. 1] (Rome, 1939), pp. 205 ff.; Laurence Lee Howe, *The Praetorian Praefect from Commodus to Diocletian* (Chicago, 1942).

the praetorian prefect had, in addition, achieved broad jurisdiction in civil and criminal cases of the private law. He had original jurisdiction of cases beyond the hundredth milestone of Rome within the confines of Italy, and he entertained both civil and criminal appeals from the decisions of the provincial governors. The civil activities had come into such prominence that in the normally collegial office one of the prefects was a man experienced in military affairs, while the other was an expert in judicial and administrative matters.

Fulvius Plautianus had been the sole occupant of the office of praetorian prefect from the date of his appointment to some time during his stay in Egypt.[96] Then his colleague was for a short time the ex-governor of Egypt. But whether he was acting as sole prefect or with a colleague, his competence was that of the office of praetorian prefect.[97] And the normal jurisdiction of that office would not extend to Comon's case, whether that case was civil or criminal or administrative or military.

The praetorian prefect's civil or criminal jurisdiction in first instance did not extend to cases arising in Rome or in Egypt. The *praefectus urbi* was the emperor's delegate in the former, and the prefect of Egypt had supreme command in the latter. It is unlikely that Comon's audacious acts were perpetrated elsewhere than in Rome, if indeed they were done at all outside of Egypt. Clearly the matter was not one of appeal from a previous decision, nor was the praetorian prefect competent in administrative hearings in Egypt. The auctions farming the taxes were held in Egypt, and, although the ultimate destination of some of the monies paid over might have been Rome, the supervision of the collection of direct as well as farmed-out taxes in Egypt rested always with the governor of the province. Finally, the prefect of Egypt was the supreme commander of the military forces in Egypt,[98] if one was to suppose that Comon was in the army. The governor further had control over military requisitions (annona militaris), besides which there

[96] The life and career of Plautianus, Stein, "Fulvius (101)," *RE*, 7, 270 ff.; Passerini, *op. cit. supra*, note 95, pp. 316 f.; Howe, *op. cit. supra*, note 95, pp. 69 f. The designation of Plautianus as *kratistos* (egregius) is a strange anomaly, for the normal title of the praetorian prefect at this time was the higher title of *exochōtatos* (eminentissimus) and for Plautianus, of consular rank, it should be *lamprotatos* (clarissimus); cf. Otto Hornickel, *Ehren- und Rangprädikate in den Papyrusurkunden* (Diss. Giessen, 1930), pp. 12, 19 ff., 22 ff.

[97] Howe, *op. cit. supra*, note 95, p. 35, argues that there is no reason to believe that Plautianus's competence was broader than that of the office of praetorian prefect; Howe, p. 35 n. 14, also considers the Columbia Comon-Apion case.

[98] Jean Lesquier, *L'Armée romaine d'Égypte d'Auguste à Dioclétien* [Mémoires . . . Institut français d'archéologie orientale du Caire, 41] (Cairo, 1918), p. 116.

was little likelihood that this form of taxation of the population was farmed out.[99]

The case was thus not within the praetorian prefect's normal jurisdiction. But there is no reason why the emperor could not specifically designate Plautianus to conduct the particular investigation. The power of the emperor to designate a judge to hear a particular case is well attested. The emperor and members of his staff were in Egypt. He himself stepped into the shoes of the prefect of Egypt, and his chancellery had temporarily taken over. There is no reason why his trusted subordinate and "companion" might not be called upon to turn his attention to a serious matter. Perhaps the practice was not unusual, for it appears the praetorian prefect who was in office accompanied Severus on his varied campaigns.[100]

Plautianus was called upon to investigate (*exetazō*) the alleged audacities of Comon. It may be said that there is no proceeding so typical of Greco-Egyptian official life as a magisterial investigation. Administrative officers were charged with looking into every conceivable matter, police proceedings were largely investigations, specific details of civil and criminal actions were assigned to subordinate magistrates for determination. It is thus impossible to designate what form of investigation Plautianus was to undertake. The implication is that it was to be criminal in nature. This rests both upon the "audacious acts" of Comon as well as upon *egklēma*, "charges," against him. The investigation, however, was not a criminal action involving court proceedings. Plautianus had no jurisdiction over criminal actions in Egypt, and the emperor has delegated him none. The conclusion is that Plautianus was to make a full investigation in order to determine the further steps to be taken in Comon's case.

Apion, the tax-farmer, was also to be investigated "if he is involved in the charges against Comon." [101] The verb employed is *koinōneō*, which generally indicates complicity in a criminal act. The nominal form *koinōnos* is

---

[99] Berchem, *Mémoires de la Société Nationale des Antiquaires de France*, 8th ser., 10 (1937), 138 ff., 154 ff., 188.

[100] There is no reason to believe that the attachment of the praetorian prefect to the residence of the emperor only became established with Diocletian, so also Howe, *op. cit. supra*, note 95, p. 9. The jurist Papinian accompanied Severus to Britain as praetorian prefect, Karlowa, *op. cit. supra*, note 2, I, 735.

[101] The verb *koinōneō* can take the genitive of the thing and the dative of the person, i.e.. "if he is involved in the charges with Comon"; the verb *egkaleō*, from which *egklēma* derives, takes the dative to denote the person against whom the charges are preferred. The second alternative is adopted here.

the equivalent of the Latin *socius*.[102] Though it may be used to designate a cocriminal, it generally has the sense of an accomplice either before or after the crime. That is the sense in which it is to be understood in this rescript. Comon is the alleged perpetrator of the criminal act; Apion may have abetted him or been implicated in some fashion. If there was any evidence of complicity, Apion was to stand investigation before Plautianus. At the conclusion of the investigation a determination would be made as to the further steps to be taken against Apion.

On the other hand, if direct criminal complicity was not evident, Isidorus was to have the prefect of Egypt as judge in the case against Apion. There can be no doubt that judicial action was contemplated. The word *dikastēs*, "judge," signifies any type of judicial magistrate; the proceeding under his control may be civil or criminal. *Dikastēs* does, however, indicate that the magistrate exercised judicial functions in the strict sense of the term. In other words, a trial and not an investigation was called for. The prefect of Egypt was the official, and the sole official in the province, in whom jurisdiction was vested by the emperor.[103] He might delegate competence to try cases to subordinate officials, and very frequently he did that, but he himself acted as judge in civil and criminal actions in Alexandria and on circuit.

The general circumstances of the case presented by the rescript might lead to the conclusion that criminal action against Apion was suggested. But the fact that Apion underwent investigation *only* if he was directly implicated with Comon implies the contrary. It should also be borne in mind that Isidorus was seeking relief. As a public-spirited citizen he may have wished to bring culprits to justice, but as a private individual he would undoubtedly seek satisfaction for the injury he has suffered. Both the Egyptian and the Roman law had long recognized what may be termed private penal actions.[104] The delicts or torts of the modern law were in those legal systems

---

[102] For complicity in the Roman criminal law, see Karl Poetzsch, *Der Begriff und die Bedeutung des socius im römischen Strafrecht* (Diss. Göttingen, 1934); cf. also, Raoul Balougditch, *Étude sur la complicite en droit pénal romain* (Diss. Montpellier, 1920).

[103] Summary discussion of his legal powers, Reinmuth, *op. cit. supra*, note 17, pp. 85 ff.; cf. also Coroi, *Actes du Vᵉ congrès international de Papyrologie, Oxford 1937* (Brussels, 1938), pp. 626 ff., with further bibliography. The limited jurisdiction conferred on the *iuridicus* by the emperor is no infringement on the governor's competence; see references in Leopold Wenger, *Institutes of the Roman Law of Civil Procedure*, trans. Otis Harrison Fisk (New York, 1940), p. 71 n. 46.

[104] The literature in the Roman law is given by Berger, *ED*, s.vv. *Crimen* and *Delictum*. For Egyptian law, see Raphael Taubenschlag, *Das Strafrecht im Rechte der Papyri* (Berlin-Leipzig, 1916), pp. 78 ff., and briefly, Taubenschlag, *Law*, pp. 325 ff. It is unfortunate that

civil actions brought by the injured person against the wrongdoer and resulted in the recovery of fines by the plaintiff, the injured party. The majority of these actions were of long standing, but the praetor in Rome might grant new types as need arose. It will be recalled that in the passage quoted from Ulpian on the audacious acts of tax-farmers, the praetor "promulgated an edict for the purpose of checking their audacity." [105] Through another edict the praetor granted a private penal action for property illegally taken by force under color of tax collection. The tax-farmer was liable whether the wrong had been committed by one of the partners in the organization or by any of its employees. The penal sum recovered was double the value of the property taken if suit was brought within a year, the single value thereafter.

In the provinces the governor exercised the same functions as the praetor in Rome. In his provincial edict he granted an action against tax-farmers for illegal taking of property.[106] The emperor in our rescript was accordingly advising Isidorus that he had a private penal action against Apion. It did not matter whether the tax-farmer himself illegally deprived the plaintiff of his money or property. It was enough if this was done by a copartner, agent, or employee of the organization. Comon was this copartner, agent, or employee. The liability of a person in the position of Apion is graphically portrayed in an extract from the writings of the jurist Modestinus, discussing a situation identical with that in the Columbia rescript. One is tempted to say that it might be the very case itself. Modestinus says: "If there are several tax-farmers who have illicitly exacted something, the action for double the value is not multiplied, but all the parties contribute and what cannot be paid by one is taken from another, as *divus* Severus and Antoninus rescripted: for they established that there is a good deal of difference between coactors in a crime and participants in the injury." [107] Professor Levy has shown that denial of multiple actions dates from the time of Severus.[108] The reason given by the emperor was that tax-farmers as such were

---

Taubenschlag does not clearly differentiate between private penal actions and public trials; cf. his note, *Law*, p. 325 n. 1.

[105] Dig. 39.4.12; *supra*, note 95. Generally on the edict of employment of force, see Otto Lenel, *Das Edictum Perpetuum* (3d ed.; Leipzig, 1927), pp. 387 ff.; Pernice, *SZ*, 5 (1884), 128 ff.

[106] Evidenced by Gaius's discussion of the edict on theft by tax collectors, in his comment on the provincial edict, book XIII (Dig. 39.4.13).

[107] Dig. 39.4.6.

[108] Ernst Levy, *Die Konkurrenz der Aktionen und Personen im klassischen römischen Recht* (Berlin, 1918), I, 489 ff. Cf. also, on this passage, Ferrini, *op. cit. supra*, note 30, pp. 285 f.

to be distinguished from joint perpetrators of crime (criminis rei) who are cumulatively liable, for the tax-farmers are but participants in the profits resulting from the injury committed (fraudis participes).   In other words, if Apion was found to be a cocriminal with Comon, both were liable to private penal actions by Isidorus for double the value, in addition to whatever public criminal punishment they might suffer.   If, however, Comon was the person who illegally exacted property from Isidorus, and Apion as his partner in the *societas publicanorum* merely benefited from the money brought into the common pool, Isidorus had but one private penal action for double the value, the satisfaction of which was shared by the partners.

This is indeed a significant rescript.   It has provided further evidence of illegal tax-farming operations in the age of the Severi.   It has thrown new light on the activities of the praetorian prefect.   Most important of all, if the interpretation of the roles of Comon and Apion are correct, and this seems to be borne out by the text, it has afforded confirmation of a complex development in the edictal action against *publicani*.

NUMBER XII

52   Ισ]ιδωρω τω και Ḥρạκλ[ειδ]ẹι [δια Α]πολλωνιου.
της πατρωας κληρονομιας αποστας και
την εκ της ηλικιας ου[κ] εχων βοηθειαν τω
νομω των πρασεων επι την ουσιαν δε-
δημευσθαι φης. πειθ[ο]υ.

To Isidorus, also called Heraclides, through Apollonius.
    Although you have given up your paternal in-
heritance and you do not have the benefit [aris-
ing] from minority status under the law of transactions, you assert that the patrimony has been
proscribed. Obey.

The twelfth rescript of the papyrus is largely a restatement of circumstances which had been set forth in the petition.   The emperor's answer is restricted to the single word, *peithou*, "obey" or "comply."   There are three situations involved in the chancellery's statement of the petitioner's case.   It is proposed to examine these in succession in order to determine the basis of the imperial decision.

From the opening clause of the rescript it is learned that the petitioner has given up (*apostas*) his paternal inheritance. In a few papyri of Greco-Roman Egypt, prominent among which is a rescript of Severus published while he was in Egypt, the same word is used to refer to an institution which may well be the Roman *cessio bonorum*, "cession of property." [109] An Augustan statute permitted an insolvent debtor to surrender his property to his creditors to escape disabilities resulting from the forced sale of his assets. Debtors in Egypt exercised the same privilege, and it was further utilized to give relief from public obligations. Giving up an inheritance in order to be free from the debts of the deceased may well be involved in this rescript, although this is not a true *cessio bonorum*. This is made clear by a papyrus of the third century. A woman renounced her brother's estate in order to escape liability for his debts.[110] As already pointed out in the comment on this papyrus, it is important to note that the woman was not a debtor; she had not yet accepted the inheritance. Similarly, in our case there was no *cessio bonorum* but rather a refusal to accept an inheritance. In a recently published papyrus of the early part of the second century, a son declared that he ceded the half of the whole heritage of his father due him in order to escape the penalties laid upon the father by the Egyptian financial administration.[111] Such abstention from inheritance (se abstinere) is well known to the Roman law. Indeed, in the late Greek corpus of that legal system, the Basilica, the technical term of our rescript is to be found.[112] Accordingly, the first point noted in the petition was that Isidorus had voluntarily relinquished his paternal inheritance.

This refusal of Isidorus to accept the inheritance was made when he was a minor, for the rescript goes on to say that the petitioner was not entitled to the benefits accorded those in minority status. There is particularly full information in the papyri as to the meaning of this part of the rescript.[113]

[109] Rescript of Severus: BGU II 473,4 = Mitteis, *Chrest.* 375. Further instances of *cessio bonorum* in the papyri cited by Taubenschlag, *Law*, p. 405 n. 23, but normally the verb employed is a form of *existēmi*, not *aphistēmi*, cf. Andreas B. Schwarz, *Die öffentliche und private Urkunden im römischen Aegypten* [Abh. d. philol.-hist. Kl. d. Sächs. Akad. d. Wissensch., 31.3] (Leipzig, 1920), pp. 219 ff.

[110] P. Ryl. II 117 = *Negotia* 181 (269 A.D.). Fritz Schulz, *Classical Roman Law* (Oxford, 1951), pp. 214 f., shows why in the Roman law the position of an heir to an inheritance encumbered with debts was not the same as that of an insolvent debtor; *cessio bonorum* was not made available to the heir who accepted the inheritance.

[111] P. Fam. Teb. 17 (117 A.D.).

[112] Bas. 10.4.7 = Dig. 4.4.7.5; Bas. 35.14.82 = Dig. 29.2.91; Bas. 41.7.17 = Dig. 37.7.8. In all a form of *aphistēmi* replaces *se abstinere* of the Digest.

[113] On the *lex Laetoria* in the papyri, see Taubenschlag, *SZ*, 37 (1916), 213 n. 2; Wenger,

A certain *lex Laetoria* of the first decade of the second century B.C. granted protection to persons who had not yet completed their twenty-fifth year of age. It provided that action could be brought against anyone who had fraudulently taken advantage of the inexperienced minor. Later the praetor permitted a restoration to status quo (restitutio in integrum) even if there had not been fraud, if the minor so requested. The papyri show that the benefits of the law and the praetor's application of it were extended to Egypt, and not only Roman citizens but the peregrine population were included. Among these texts two rescripts of Severus were posted in Alexandria during his stay in Egypt which, if they had been taken advantage of, afforded relief to minors.[114] These rescripts employ exactly the same phraseology—without the negation—that is to be found in our rescript. The chancellery had clearly a set formula for use when occasion demanded.

The phrase, "under the law of sales" literally translated, occurs immediately following the statement denying the benefits of minority status. The writer believes that this phrase relates to the benefits afforded by the *lex Laetoria* and that it is not to be connected with the words that follow. There is no reference in the papyri to any "law of sales" earlier than the age of Justinian.[115] The word *prasis*, however, can have a general meaning of "agreement" or "transaction." It is suggested that the *lex Laetoria* might have been referred to as a "law of transactions" inasmuch as it was the legal transactions of the minor which could be invalidated.[116]

The petitioner had undoubtedly changed his mind and wished now to enter into the inheritance in spite of the debts or other obligations which may have been outstanding. In this respect a minor could change his mind. But the benefits of the *lex Laetoria* ceased with the completion of his twenty-fifth year. The petition was actually made by an agent, but there is no reason to suppose that Apollonius was a guardian (curator) of Isidorus and that the latter was still a minor. Apollonius might at one time have been a guardian, but the address in this rescript permits us to say only that he

---

Quellen, p. 818 n. 937. For the Roman law, references in Berger, *ED*, s.v. *Lex Plaetoria* (? *Laetoria*). On the name, Schulz, *op. cit. supra*, note 110, p. 191.

[114] P. Oxy. VII 1020 = Meyer, *Jur. Pap.* 17 (199/200 A.D.).

[115] Taubenschlag, "*Nomos* in the Papyri," *JJP*, 2 (1948), 67 ff., has collected all the references and notes only occurrences in P. Mon. I, p. 56.

[116] Huschke, *Zeitschrift für Rechtsgeschichte*, 13 (1878), 314 ff., would limit the benefits of minority status to obligations and property alienations and would exclude delicts and testamentary transactions; cf. Weiss, "Lex Plaetoria," *RE*, Supp. 5, 578.

was the representative of the petitioner. The most likely basis for the denial of the benefits of minority status by the emperor is that the age of twenty-five had been passed.

The major point made in the petition was the assertion, to use the words of the rescript, "that the patrimony (*epi* [!] *tēn ousian*) had been proscribed (*dēmeusthai*)." [117] *Ousia* refers to the property, specifically "patrimony," which constituted the inheritance. The word *demeuō* is not common in the papyri, though in contemporary Greek writings it frequently has the sense of "confiscate." Confiscation by the state is what is meant, more particularly by the fisc, as punishment for a crime. In the papyrological sources such confiscation is regularly expressed by the word *analambanō*. In the bilingual glosses, admittedly of later date, *dēmeuō* is equated with *proscribo* and *publico* as well as with *confisco*.[118] All three have the general meaning of taking property, but the first two emphasize the sale thereof. If an attempt is made to reconstruct the events recorded in the rescript, the first of the three terms seems preferable. Isidorus presumably declined to accept the inheritance in the first place because it was overburdened with outstanding debts. As heir these would be his responsibility. Since no other heir or intestate successor appeared, the creditors would seek to have the estate sold in order that their claims might be satisfied. Application was made—to the praetor in Rome and to the governor in the provinces—for an order granting possession and for leave to post public notices (proscribere) advertising the forthcoming sale of the property of the deceased. About this time Isidorus realized that he might have been hasty, and so he sought to halt the sale.

It is not suggested that the measures taken in Rome for the sale of in-debted estates were identical with those followed in Egypt.[119] In the latter country sale by auction had long been a common method of satisfying the claims of private individuals or claims of the state. The practice of publicly advertising the sale was a preliminary step. There is no reason to infer that any attempt was being made to impose the details of the Roman forced sale upon the Egyptian system. The words of the rescript indicate merely that the normal procedure was to be followed. In drafting the answer the bureau

[117] The construction with *epi* seems grammatically incorrect.

[118] CGL VI-VII, Indices, s.vv. *confisco, proscribo, publico*.

[119] Gaius, Inst. 3,78 ff., describes the procedure of the public sale of the assets of living persons (bankrupts) and of dead persons (indebted estates). For Egypt, see Pringsheim, "The Greek Sale by Auction," *Scritti in onore di Contardo Ferrini* (Milan, 1949), IV, 284 ff., which treats simultaneously of the institution in Greece, Ptolemaic and Roman Egypt. On the counterpart of *proscriptio*, p. 295 n. 2.

a libellis naturally employed the accepted Latin tag, *bona proscribere*, to signify the procedure as a whole. The translation of this expression into Greek was perfectly understandable to the Egyptians, while perhaps not technically descriptive of the practice observed. Steps were being taken to sell the estate; the emperor emphatically declared that there was to be no interference with the normal procedure. Whether the petitioner was involved personally in any of the measures cannot be determined, but this might be intimated through the use of the imperative *peithou*, "obey" or "comply." In any event the petitioner had his answer: he cannot reverse his former action and accept the inheritance. The benefits of minority status were no longer available to him. And the procedure of disposing of the property of the deceased was to continue in normal fashion.

NUMBER XIII

57
.[.]ελαθηω Καιρενου.
εαν τοις ορφανοις επιτροπους λ[α]βης
εξωθεν ταξεως υπερ των χωριων προς τους
νεμομενους δικαστης δοθησεται.

To . .elatheus, son of Caerenus.
If you take guardians for the orphans
extra ordinem, a judge will be given with
respect to their properties against those
in possession.

The final rescript in the papyrus is presented in conditional form and therefore affords an opportunity for commenting upon it in two parts. The translation of the protasis of the condition is clear but the substance of the statement is obscure. This is due to the uncertainty of the status of the addressee and the significance of the phrase *exōthen taxeōs*, a direct translation of the Latin *extra ordinem*. A brief résumé of the Roman law of guardianship will, it is believed, provide a basis for the answer of the two questions.[120] Whether we are here concerned with Roman law or with local law is a question which can be left open for the time being.

[120] A recent comprehensive study by Sachers, "Tutela," *RE*, 7A, 1497–1599, affords an excellent treatment with extensive bibliography, 1502 f. A good short résumé by Schulz, *op. cit. supra*, note 110, pp. 162 ff.

In early Republican times Roman law knew two kinds of guardians. First there was the *tutor legitimus*, the nearest male heir of a Roman who died intestate or whose will was invalid, and who left minor children. Second there was the *tutor testamentarius*, the guardian named in the will. In the second century B.C. a *lex Atilia* provided that if an infant in Rome lacked a tutor one was to be named by the *praetor urbanus* with the assistance of the tribunes. This provision was extended to the provinces by a *lex Iulia* and *Titia*, perhaps two laws of the last century of the Republic. The governor was entrusted with the naming of a guardian for a Roman minor who was without one. A marked change in the law of guardianship occurred when the emperor Claudius decreed, as Suetonius tells us, "that guardians were given *extra ordinem* to infants by the consuls." [121] From that time on the consuls played a significant role in guardianship affairs. Not only did they supplement the praetor in the power of appointment of guardians, but they altered the whole nature of the institution. A guardian named by consular authority had to serve unless excused for recognized cause and had to give security for the protection of the interests of the minor. A guardian who neglected his duties was subject to severe penalties and might also be replaced. Some scholars hold that neither a *tutor legitimus* nor *tutor testamentarius* nor —and here all agree—a guardian appointed by praetor or consul could lay down the guardianship without permission.[122] The key to the change in the nature of the institution seems to be contained in the phrase *extra ordinem*.

As Professor Solazzi has shown, the jurist Ulpian is speaking of the consuls when he states, "a tutor is wont to be compelled *extra ordinem* to conduct and administer a guardianship." [123] In this instance *extra ordinem* does not refer to the well-known distinction between the new procedure of the Principate and the traditional formulary procedure known as the *ordo iudiciorum*. Nor does it indicate an exceptional case. It refers to the extraordinary, supplemental, source of authority provided by *senatus consulta* and imperial enactments and exercised by the emperor and his officials.[124] It is similar, for example, to the reference in the Digest to criminal trials

---

[121] Suetonius, Claudius 23.

[122] For the diversity of opinion on the so-called *abdicatio tutelae*, see Sachers, *RE*, 7A, 1532 ff.

[123] Dig. 26.7.1 pr. Siro Solazzi, *Istituti tutelari* (Naples, 1929), pp. 35 ff. Solazzi's position of the role of the consuls is generally accepted, see Pietro Bonfante, *Corso di diritto romano*, *I*: *Diritto di famiglia* (Rome, 1925), p. 403 n. 1; Paul Jörs-Wolfgang Kunkel, *Römisches Privatrecht* (3d ed.; Berlin-Göttingen-Heidelberg, 1949), p. 300 n. 3; Arangio-Ruiz, *op. cit. supra*, note 71, p. 493 n. 2.

[124] This view was first broached by Hartmann-Ubbelohde, *op. cit. supra*, note 81, pp. 470 ff.

"which punish [either] in accordance with statutes or *extra ordinem*." [125]
The administrative functions with respect to guardianship were therefore
broadened by the "extraordinary" powers conferred by *senatus consulta* or
imperial enactments, far beyond that provided by the laws of the time of the
Republic. On the other hand, there was little change in the private law side
of the institution, that is, in suits between guardian and ward or between
coguardians, all of which was still largely governed by the edict of the praetor
in Rome or by that of the governor in the provinces.

The practice of appointing additional tutors for a ward (tutores adiuncti),
if deemed necessary, flowed from authority conferred *extra ordinem*.[126] A
temporary tutor might be named if the regular tutor was unable to carry on
if, for example, he was absent on state business, was incapacitated by mental
or physical illness, or was taken captive. Additional tutors were appointed
if the ward's estate was considerably enlarged during the period of its administration. Then again, it was a rule that a guardian was not required to
administer the estate of a ward if it was in a region remote from his residence.
Additional tutors were named to administer the property apart. Such was
the status of the supervision of guardianship as presented in Roman legal
sources.

The papyri of Roman Egypt have given us a fairly complete picture of
the way in which guardians were appointed and their activities supervised
in the province.[127] The appointment of tutors for the peregrine population
was made by subordinate local officials; this was a continuation of practices
of pre-Roman times. The governor was empowered to name a tutor for
Roman infants who had no *tutor legitimus* or *tutor testamentarius*, by virtue
of the *lex Iulia* and *Titia*. This function could be delegated to a subordinate
official and the investigation of the suitability of the person selected to act
as guardian turned over to local magistrates. Several petitions for the

---

Accepted by Paul Jörs, *Untersuchungen zur Gerichtsverfassung der römischen Kaiserzeit* (Leipzig, 1892), p. 4 n. 5, and by Solazzi, *loc. cit. supra*, note 123. Though all authorities are today
agreed that Hartmann's theory of the nature of the *cognitio* procedure is erroneous, this does
not disprove his explanation of the significance of *extra ordinem* in the texts.

[125] Cod. 3.15.1 (196 A.D.); cf. also Dig. 4.6.2 pr.

[126] Instances of appointment of supplementary tutors given by Sachers, *RE*, 7A, 1524 f.,
1578 f. Among these note, exemption from guardianship when task is in a remote locale:
Dig. 26.7.39.7; 27.1.21.2; Cod. 5.34.5; 5.62.2; Vat. Frag. 203. For cases involving supplementary guardians where property to be administered is remote: Dig. 26.2.15; 26.5.27 pr.;
26.7.3.4; 26.7.3.9 + 4; 26.7.51; 46.3.100; Cod. 5.36.3; 5.62.11.1; Vat. Frag. 232.

[127] Mitteis, *SZ*, 29 (1908), 390 ff.; Oertel, *op. cit. supra*, note 88, pp. 405 ff.

naming of guardians have been preserved with direct reference to the authority provided by the *lex Iulia* and *Titia*.[128]

The governor also exercised general supervision over the administration of guardianship, an authority flowing from the powers described above as *extra ordinem*. There is nothing remarkable in this for it has long been recognized that he combined in his person the two aspects of Roman authority, namely, the traditional jurisdiction exercised by the praetor in Rome as well as the competence of a delegate of the emperor.[129] The prefect could delegate this administrative supervision to subordinates in Egypt. In a papyrus of the middle of the second century we read of an action against testamentary tutors who have neglected the interests of the minors, and of their subsequent replacement by new guardians.[130] In another document there is a petition for excuse from guardianship on the ground that the property of the ward was outside Antinoopolis and the petitioner, an Antinoopolite, was therefore not obliged to undertake this obligation.[131] Precedents cited in this papyrus and other documents indicate that a high Roman official, a delegate of the governor, heard these cases and that the subordinate local officials who are mentioned merely acted as investigating authorities. The important factor to be pointed out in this administrative phase of guardianship is that matters which fall within the *extra ordinem* authority of the Roman officials concern the welfare of both Roman and non-Roman minors. That is the reason, finally made clear, why emphasis has been placed on Roman law in the discussion of this rescript. The petitioner is clearly not a Roman citizen as his name and patronym indicate, yet in the matter of guardianship he appeals to the highest authority, that of the emperor.

The conclusion may be drawn that the supervision over guardians is in the strictest sense neither a matter of Roman law nor of local Egyptian law. If Greeks or Egyptians sought guardians where minors had none, application was made to the local officials; this is local Egyptian, folk law. If Roman minors failed to be provided with a *tutor legitimus* or *tutor testamentarius*, a

[128] For example, P. Oxy. IV 720 = Meyer, *Jur. Pap.* 13 = *Negotia* 24 (247 A.D.); Diptych, ed. Grenfell, *Bodleian Quarterly Record*, 1919, 259 = SB 6223 = *Negotia* 25 (198 A.D.). Cf. Wenger, *Quellen*, p. 819 n. 954.

[129] Adolf Friedrich Rudorff, *Über den liber de officio proconsulis* [Abh. d. Akad. d. Wissensch. zu Berlin, philos.-hist. Kl.] (Berlin, 1865), pp. 243 f.; Karlowa, *op. cit. supra*, note 2, I, 571; Balogh, *Atti del congresso internazionale di diritto romano, Roma 1933* (Pavia, 1935), II, 297.

[130] P. Catt. vo. I, 25 ff., II, 10–III, 26 = Mitteis, *Chrest.* 88 (c. 150 A.D.).

[131] P. Mich. Inv. No. 2922, ed. A. E. R. Boak, *JEA*, 18 (1932), 69 = SB 7558 = *Negotia* 30 = *Select Papyri* 260 (172–173 A.D.).

guardian was named by virtue of the *lex Iulia* and *Titia*; this is Roman *ius civile*. But the administrative control of guardians, including the naming of supplementary guardians, rests on the *extra ordinem* powers; this is imperial law (*Reichsrecht*), or at least provincial law (*Provinzialrecht*), and is thus of general application to all.[132] The phrase *exōthen taxeōs* not only adds to the sparse number of references to *extra ordinem* in connection with the supervision of guardianship in the time of the late Principate, but it affords further insight into the extent of imperial law in Egypt before the *constitutio Antoniniana*.

Turning now to the Columbia rescript, it is clear that the petitioner cannot be concerned with "taking" guardians for minors who have no other guardian. The orphans were not Romans, for in that case such an application would be in Latin. Application for the naming of a first guardian for Greco-Egyptian infants would be directed to a local official, not to the emperor nor to the prefect of Egypt. This fact excludes from consideration a number of persons as possible petitioners. The addressee cannot be a male relative seeking to protect the rights of infants without a guardian, nor creditors nor other persons interested in the estate of the orphans. A clue is provided in a phrase in the concluding portion of the rescript, *hyper chōriōn*, "with respect to the properties." The problem put to the emperor thus concerned *tutores adiuncti*, "supplementary tutors," needed for the care of property of the orphans outside the residence of the acting guardian. The petitioner was, consequently, the existing guardian. It cannot be said whether he was testamentary tutor or statutory tutor or guardian named by a magistrate. His wards were the orphans mentioned (*orphanoi*, pupilli). If called upon to undertake the administration of the property which was away from his residence, he would if he wished be entitled to be excused.[133] The request to the emperor may thus have been a plea to be excused from the wards' affairs. The emperor's answer then would indicate the manner in which the matter could be correctly handled, namely, the designation of *tutores adiuncti* with the regular guardian continuing to administer the affairs of the orphans in his own locale. On the other hand, the guardian-petitioner might be con-

---

[132] In addition to the two mentioned above, among the papyri on guardianship illustrating the exercise of *extra ordinem* powers may be included: P. Rend. Harr. 68 = *Negotia* 28 (225 A.D.), petition to *iuridicus*, representative of prefect; P. Merton 26 (274 A.D.); P. Geneva, ed. Nicole-Wilcken, *AP*, 3 (1906), 370 ff. Generally, on the distinction between *Reichsrecht* and *Provinzialrecht*, both distinct from *Volksrecht*, see Schönbauer, *SZ*, 57 (1937), 349 ff.

[133] A guardian could voluntarily undertake to administer estates in another nome than his own, see P. Rend. Harr. 68, *cit.* note 132.

templating or already have taken supplementary guardians, and thus he was merely seeking information about the further course of conduct. The second alternative is preferred for the language of the rescript is not framed as an answer to an application for excuse from guardianship.

The reason for a plurality of *tutores adiuncti* is not evident.[134] It does not seem that a number of tutors were proposed because the properties were in different nomes. Perhaps the guardian desired *contutores* in the handling of the remote property to better protect the interests of the orphans. In case of maladministration on their part, any one of the *tutores adiuncti* can be sued and recovery had to the full extent of the damage.

A final point raised by an expression in the protasis of the condition needs brief mention. The expression is "take guardians." Whether the naming of a first guardian or of supplementary guardians by magisterial action, the technical wording is *epitropon kathistēmi, tutorem dare,* "to give a guardian." In our rescript the matter is looked at from the point of view of the petitioner. The expression is clearly nontechnical, but it permits of no ambiguity. It has its counterpart in the expression *iudicem accipere,* "to take a judge," [135] when a superior official delegates a subordinate to hear a case, *iudicem dare,* an instance of which as we shall shortly see is presented in this very rescript.

The apodosis of the condition in this rescript raises three problems: (1) what type of judge is meant, (2) what is the nature of the process, and (3) who are the defendants. The source of judicial authority in Egypt, as has been noted earlier, was the *praefectus Aegypti,* the governor of the province. He could hear cases himself or delegate his authority to subordinate magistrates. Such delegation of judicial authority was normally described as *kritēn didōmi, iudicem dare,* "to give a judge." The judge so designated was, of course, the *iudex datus* of the Latin sources, the judge functioning in the magisterial procedure of the provinces or in the *cognitio* procedure in Rome during the late classical epoch. Sometimes in the papyri the word *dikastēs,* "judge," is substituted for *kritēs;* both mean a magistrate acting in judicial capacity. In the Greek constitutions of the Codex Iustinianus, *dikastēs* is more frequently employed than *kritēs,* which may point to the fact that even in the time of the Severi the imperial bureaus would use *dikastēn dothēsetai* as a translation of *iudicem dabitur,* "a judge will be given." The meaning is

---

[134] On *contutores* and their liability, Sachers, *RE,* 7A, 1526 f., 1551 ff., 1575 ff.

[135] Moriz Wlassak, *Zum römischen Provinzialprozess* [Sitzb. d. Akad. d. Wissensch. in Wien, philos.-hist. Kl., 190.4] (Vienna, 1919), p. 25 n. 25.

that a magistrate will be delegated to hear a case, presumably a civil rather than a criminal trial.

The case to be heard concerns real property. It is suggested that this property was claimed as part of the estate of the orphans, but at the moment it was not in their possession. The law of Roman Egypt provided a number of methods for recovering the possession of property withheld from the rightful owners. But the words of this rescript are too meager to suggest more than that the supplemental tutors were to institute action for recovery of the property. That action would be directed "against those in possession." The word *nemō* has an original meaning of "distribute," but in the course of time it took on the significance of "possess," particularly in the middle voice. It displays both meanings in the papyri and in contemporary Greek literature. Consequently, "against those (to whom something is) distributed," or "against those (to whom the guardianship is) assigned" might be possible translations. But it is difficult to reconstruct a suit by the one guardian against the *contutores* which would concern real property. There is no mention of irregularities on the part of the *tutores adiuncti*. Even if an *accusatio tutoris suspecti*, an action against a guardian for maladministration, were meant, the subject of the suit would not be "properties." [136] It would be an action by the one guardian against the others for their wrongful or negligent acts. The context thus indicates that "against those (who are) possessing" is to be preferred, a suit against the present possessors of the "properties" claimed by the orphans.

In conclusion, the answer given by the emperor permits of the following reconstruction of the situation. A guardian, acting in the interests of his wards, wished to recover possession of property which had been wrongfully occupied by other persons. The property was situated in a locale other than that of his own residence, and he was therefore unable to institute and carry through the necessary litigation. He petitioned the emperor in order to be informed of the proper measures to be taken. He was told by the rescript that if he requested supplemental tutors resident in that locality, as the imperial law permitted, these tutors could in normal fashion apply for the designation of a judge to hear the case. Suit could be brought against the persons in the possession of the property in the name of and in the interests of the wards.

---

[136] On this action, consult Sachers, *RE*, 7A, 1556 ff. The papyrus referred to earlier, P. Catt. vo., note 130, is an instance of this action in Egypt.

THE SCRIBE'S INTENTION

A FINAL CONCLUSION to legal comment on a single papyrus is seldom if ever expected. This is not the occasion to evaluate the significance of the individual rescripts in the fields of law to which they pertain nor is it the time to deal with the effect upon the legal system of the emperor's visit to Egypt. A minor, perhaps one might say a much more humble topic, has engaged the attention of the writer and this may serve to close this comment. Originally it seemed that the problem was a legal one. Further study has led to a different conclusion. The question can be simply stated. What exactly impelled the scribe to make a transcript of the thirteen rescripts which comprise P. Columbia 123?

Collections of imperial enactments in published papyri are not infrequent. There are instances in which a number of imperial constitutions all dealing with the same subject were gathered together to serve as memoranda for the future.[137] More frequently, imperial enactments together with prefectural decisions were cited as support for a petition or as precedents in a trial.[138] Here again all the documents dealt with a single topic. The Columbia papyrus is clearly not of this type. There could scarcely be a more varied array of subject matter than that offered by the thirteen rescripts. A few published papyri show that significant constitutions on different topics were combined within a single document at some time subsequent to the date of their proclamation.[139] The Columbia papyrus, on the other hand, was transcribed from official texts which had just been posted. There was nothing of tremendous import in the texts which were copied. To the writer's knowledge there is one other document only which is possibly of similar nature to P. Columbia 123. That papyrus is P. Amherst 63. This contains a version of the second of the Columbia subscripts together with another largely illegible text which was posted six days later. This papyrus is by a different scribe although the purpose it was intended to serve may have been similar.[140]

---

[137] Good examples are P. Oxy. VII 1020, *cit. supra*, note 114; P. Strassb. 22, *cit. supra*, note 61. Cf. generally, Reinmuth, *Classical Philology*, 31 (1936), 151 n. 2.

[138] A typical example is P. Teb. II 286 = *Negotia* 100 (time of Hadrian), referred to early in this comment, *supra*, note 12.

[139] Three edicts of Caracalla, P. Giss. I 40 = Mitteis, *Chrest.* 377–378 (212 and 215 A.D.); two *orationes* of Claudius, BGU II 611 = Mitteis, *Chrest.* 370 = *Leges* 44 (42–54 A.D.).

[140] The assumption must be made that the second text deals with a different subject and

The Columbia papyrus is neither a memorandum nor collection of precedents on a single topic and is not a compilation of earlier enacted constitutions. It might be suggested that the transcript was made for official purposes. But it could scarcely have been prepared for posting in the Fayyum where the papyrus appears to have been found, for we know that rescripts were posted at the residence of the emperor only. If these copied rescripts were destined for archives elsewhere than in Alexandria, they are deficient in form in that they lack the petitions to which the subscripts were appended and omit the emperors' names and titles as well as the notice of posting which would be required of official copies. The Columbia papyrus was evidently not a duplicate for official use.

Suppose the copies were made for a group of petitioners who resided in the Fayyum. Time and effort in the voyage to Alexandria would be obviated if a single document were prepared. But the suggestion is unlikely in view of the relatively large number of petitions that would then stem from the same locality and all answered at the same time. The possibility of the preparation of a transcript for petitioners coming to Alexandria at a later date after the rescripts had been removed to the archives and thus more difficult of access, seems also excluded because then it is difficult to explain exactly how the papyrus came to be found in the Fayyum.

It has been suggested that P. Columbia 123 was prepared for the use of an up-country judge or lawyer in order to serve as a memorandum of possible precedents for future cases.[141] This suggestion seems plausible if it can also be taken for granted that he was charged with copying all the posted rescripts. At least four of the thirteen rescripts would be of no value to the judge or lawyer as precedents. Further, many of the others would be difficult to interpret without the factual background provided by the petition. In view of the large proportion of special rescripts and the fact that scores of rescripts must have been posted during Severus's stay in Egypt, it is difficult to believe that a scribe would be given a commission to prepare a document like the Columbia papyrus.

---

that the two were transcribed at the same time to present a situation identical with that of the Columbia papyrus. P. Amh. II 63 is now in the J. P. Morgan Library, New York, where the script was compared.

[141] Westermann, *Bulletin de la Société Royale d'Archéologie d'Alexandrie*, No. 38 (1949), pp. 10 f., and *supra*, p. 5.

The writer offers the suggestion that the papyrus was a memorandum prepared by a notary for his own use. The posted rescripts afforded an excellent opportunity to procure samples of the modes of expression employed by the imperial chancellery. As has been indicated repeatedly, the technical language of these rescripts was not the Greek usage common in Egypt. To a scribe connected with an administrative bureau in the Fayyum these expressions would be of considerable value for they might be employed in the drafting of documents for the strategus or for some other local official.[142] A form sheet for a notary would explain the inclusion of a brief subscript such as "Obey the findings made" as well as the detailed answer in the Comon-Apion case. It might account also for the omission of the emperors' names and titles and the notices of posting. This hypothesis is one among many possibilities. If it should be true, one could not fail to feel a sense of deep gratitude to a scribe who, in serving his own purposes, provided so invaluable a text for posterity.

[142] See, for example, Taubenschlag, "Les Publications du stratege dans l'Égypte greco-romain," *JJP*, 5 (1951), 155 ff.

INDICES

GREEK INDEX

References in boldface type refer to lines of the text;
references in ordinary type refer to pages of the volume.

INDEX OF NAMES

Septimius Severus, **2-4**
 Αὐτοκράτωρ Καῖσαρ Λούκιος Σεπτίμιος
 Σηουῆρος Εὐσεβὴς Περτίναξ Ἀραβικὸς
 Ἀδιαβηνικὸς Παρθικὸς Μέγιστος Σεβασ-
 τός
Caracalla, **4**
 Αὐτοκράτωρ Καῖσαρ Μάρκος Αὐρήλιος
 Ἀντωνεῖνος Σεβαστός
Fulvius Plautianus, **47**
 Φλούειος Πλαυδίανος

 ⸻

Αβδομανχος, **18**, 8, 17 f.
Αβδομασιαμος, 18
Αμβρηλος, **18**, 17 f.
Αμβρος, 18
Ἀμρίλιος, 18
Ἀνουβίων, **11**
Ἀπίων, **49**, 14, 23, 82 ff.
Ἀπόλλων, **22**, 67
Ἀπολλώνιος, **28**
Ἀπολλώνιος, **52**, 8, 90
Αρνεκτωτος, **22**
Ἀρτεμίδωρος, **8**, 8, 16, 45, 55
Ἀρτεμίδωρος, **11**, 5
Αὐρήλιος, **11**, 56
Αὐρήλιος, **25**, 70
Ἀχιλλεύς, **8**, 8, 16, 45

Δεῖος, 45
Διόσκορος, **41**, 8

Ἡρακλείδης, **35**

Ἡρακλείδης, **52**
Ἡφαιστίων, **41**

Ἰσίδωρος, **45**, 23
Ἰσίδωρος, **52**, 89 ff.

Καιρένος, **57**
Καλλίνεικος, **5**, 50
Κιλ . . . δις, **13**, 8, 17
Κόμων, **46**, **50**, 13 f., 23, 82 ff.
Κρόνιος, **35**

Μίδας, **13**

Ὄσιρις, **41**
Οὔλπιος Ἡράκλανος, **5**, 15, 50, 54, 70

Πιεσῆις, **41**, 22
Πρόκλος, **28**, 74

Σαραπίων, **25**, 70

Φιλοκράτης, **13**, 17

. . ελαθηος, **57**
. . . θαλγη, **18**, 8, 17 f.

 ⸻

Αἰγύπτιος, **6**, 24
Ἀλεξάνδρεια, Title
Ἀλεξανδρεύς, **6**

 ⸻

(ἔτος) η, **2**
Φαμενώθ ιη, **2**

INDEX OF WORDS

αἴτησις, 67
ἄλλος, **11**, **19**, **22**, **42**, 4, 5
ἀναλαμβάνω, 91
ἀνατρέπω, **14**, 59
ἀνίημι, **7**
ἀντί, **43**
ἀντίγραφον, **1**, 4, 13
ἀντίχρησις, 58

ἀξιόω, **15**, 59
ἀπαλλάσσω, **36-37**
ἀπάτη, 24
ἀπό, 46
ἀπόκριμα, **1**, 4, 13, 23 n. 33, 26, 29, 30, 34,
 37, 39, 42 ff.
ἀποκρίνω, 42
ἀπόκρισις, 42

μέμφομαι, **10**, 8, 16
μέτοχος, **82**
μή, **49**
μητρόπολις, 30
μητρῷος, **26**

νέμω, **60**, 98
νομή, **16**, **30**, 61
νομοθεσία, 12 n. 8
νόμος, **55**
νόσος, **36**, 22 n. 29

οἰκεῖος, **38**, 48
ὁμοίως, **21**, **40**, 8
ὀρφανός, **58**, 96
οὐ (οὐκ), **15**, **20**, **30**, **36**, **54**
οὐσία, **55**, 71, 91
οὕτως, **15**

παρέχω, **23**
πατρῷος, **53**
πείθω, **12**, **56**, 4, 5, 16, 88, 92
περί, **23**
πίστις, **58**
πολιτικός, **36**, 80
πρᾶγμα, **33**, **38**
πρᾶσις, **14**, **55**, 17, 57, 90
πρόνοια, **24**
πρός, **17**, **49**, **59**, 5, 61
προσάγω, **7**, 15, 53
πρόσκαιρος, **36**
προτίθημι, **21**, 13, 16, 42
πρώην, **27**, 20

πυρός, **43**

στεφανικὸν ἀρχόντων, 32
στοά, **1**, **21**
στρατόπεδον, **48**
συγγραφὴ ἀποστασίου, 24
συγκατατίθημι, **9**, 16
σύμβασις, **16**, 63
σῶμα, **37**
τάξις, **34**, **59**, 77, 92
τελέω, **30**, 75
τελώνης, **49**, 82
τίθημι, **1**, 5, 42
τολμάω, **46**, 83

υἱός, **13**, **18**
ὑπάλλαγμα, 58 f.
ὑπέρ, **19**, **59**, 5, 96
ὑπογραφή, 39, 44
ὑποθήκη, **14-15**, 57 ff., 62
ὑπόλογος, 20

φημί, **56**
φροντίζω, **31**, 4
φροντίς, **38**

χρόνιος, 22 n. 29
χρόνος, **7**, 8, 13, 15, 53 f.
χωρίον, **17**, **59**, 17, 96
χωρίς, **16**, 63

ὠνὴ ἐν πίστει, 58
ὥρπερ, **14**, 8

GENERAL INDEX

References are to pages.

ACKNOWLEDGMENTS

THE EDITORS acknowledge with gratitude the generosity shown by the following in making the publication of the Bicentennial Editions and Studies possible: the Trustees of Columbia University, the Trustees of the Columbia University Press, Mrs. W. Murray Crane, Mr. James Grossman, Mr. Herman Wouk, and friends of the late Robert Pitney, who wish to remain anonymous.